YOU'RE NOT SPECIAL; YOU'RE GIFTED

BY CHAD W. GARRETT

Published by Forerunner Publications

Forerunner Publications is a Forerunner Productions, LLC subsidiary.

For Kyle;

*Who showed me what it meant
to be a Godly man.*

Work hard, play harder.

ON THE SHOULDERS OF GIANTS

"One of the saddest things I've discovered is that you need a tombstone. People who are successful don't need tombstones. The reason why we need tombstones is because we were so useless on Earth that wherever they planted us they had to mark the spot; to remind us that you used to be here."
- Dr. Miles Monroe

You're not special. You saw it on the cover. You picked up the book anyway, but I feel like I need to remind you of this.

You are not special.

I grew up, like many of you who will read this book, in a society where we were told that we're special. That we deserve whatever we want and that everyone is special and that everyone gets a trophy. I hate to break it to you, but it's not true. The number of truly special people in this world is:

1) Extremely subjective
2) Could still be numbered on a person's fingers and toes.

People like Martin Luther King Jr., Joan of Arc, C.S.

Lewis, William Shakespeare, Agatha Christie, Albert Einstein, Johan Sebastian Bach, Mahatma Gandhi, and most of all, Jesus Himself; they aren't you and me. We're nowhere close. As a matter of fact, I'm going to share a secret with you: we will never get close.

At this point, just over 200 words into the essay, you're probably ready to fold the front cover back over the book and set it on the shelf, because you don't need some random guy beating up your personal image more than you already do yourself. Now, if you haven't closed the book yet, you're probably wondering, "How in the Lord's Holy name did this book get labeled 'Self-help' and 'Motivation'?!" The answer is simple.

You're not special. You're gifted.

Now you're probably thinking, "That's contradictory!" No, it's not, and if you'll open your heart and mind to the words on these pages, I'm sure you'll walk away from this with a new perspective. Just like I did when the principles sank in after God finally beat me over the head with them 5,000 times!

TRIGGER WARNING

One of my favorite books is *Sun Stand Still* by Steven Furtick. I also tend to refer to the author as, "my spirit animal when it comes to public speaking." I aspire to his level of energy and command of stage and audience alike.

At the beginning of this particular book, Steven issues a warning. Though the book and subject matter are quite different, I want to take a note from him and issue one myself.

This book will not coddle you. I have no intention of beating around the bush or sparing your feelings. Most of you reading this have your self-image built on a foundation of trash that shifts with the blowing wind. I want to break down that foundation, and everything you have built on it, and then help you rebuild on a foundation that matters. It will not be easy. It will not feel good, at least not at first, but if you buy in to the premise you will not only be happier, you'll be more productive, and your life will inherently be more meaningful.

Some of you are hooked. I love it. Welcome to the wild ride.

Some of you think I'm full of crap. Fine. You have two options:

1) Keep reading to verify your assumptions. Maybe I'll change your mind. (This is the recommended option.)

2) Put the book down and write me off as an over-zealous, idealistic kook.

I rather enjoy the thought of talking to someone that makes it through this book and still concludes the latter.

For those who feel like this is a breath of fresh air, who are ready to be challenged, who want to grow and develop on a stronger foundation, or are just here for the 'LOLZ', I appreciate you. At the very least this will be entertaining, but I hope you pull the message from it too.

I would also like to take this moment to give a disclaimer. I am a Christian. Some of the principles within this book are inspired by my faith. At times, I will speak on things from a perspective of my faith. I did not write this book for only a Christian audience; I wrote this for anyone and everyone so that they might glean wisdom from its pages. If the idea of learning good, moral principle that could help change and improve your life becomes repugnant because the principles are inspired by a Christian worldview, this is your chance; close the book, put it down, and walk away. However, if you are of a critically-thinking mind, as I have faith that you are, then I have no doubt that you will be able to analyze the sound teachings regardless of their inspiration and origin.

If it's any consolation, I wasn't always a Christian. I passionately believe that had I never converted, I would still have come these same conclusions about each of these principles. Why? Because you can logic your way to the same conclusion if you're willing to look through an objective lens. I implore you to adopt that lens as you read this book.

THE WEALTHIEST PLACE ON EARTH

"What is the wealthiest place on earth? It is the cemetery."

-Dr. Miles Monroe

If you couldn't tell, I draw a lot of inspiration from the late doctor. God rest his soul. The first time I heard this speech, I was in technical training for the United States Air Force and in the process of crafting a Leadership Development program for the squadron I was a part of as an Airman Leader. I meant it to be inspiring and for it to ignite a similar flame for leadership in my peers as it had for me.

It fell flat. Fizzled. Died like anyone dumb enough to invade Russia in the winter. Nothing that I implemented in my time there still exists. The culture in that squadron is so different now, I couldn't begin to explain it.

It was a complete waste of time... or was it?

If all you look at is your success ratio, if all you're focused on is the measurable demographic of lives you've touched, or how many people attribute their lessons to you, or how much money you make, or how long something lasts that you've created, you're missing the point. Quit doing that. You're not special, and neither am I.

The reason that none of those things matter is that they're all fake measurements. Not a single one of those items, no matter how large the number, how broad an audience you feel like you've reached, will ever satisfy you. Craving those numbers is just another form of gluttony. Why? Because not a single one of those things can measure your *gifts*.

In the speech that I quoted earlier by Dr. Miles Monroe, the doctor goes on to explain why the cemetery is the wealthiest place.

It's because everyone is given gifts.

Now, I choose to believe that we're given our gifts by God. You can choose to believe that they come from wherever you please. However, we at least have to agree that all people, regardless of size, shape, age, race, intelligence, political affiliation, *whatever*, have all been given gifts. Society, and culture, teach us that it's dangerous for us to use our gifts. It tells us to conform to the collective rather than embrace your individuality. Maybe college isn't for you? Society wouldn't tell you that. Maybe you're good with your hands and not with a standardized test? Your peers might look at you sideways for not getting great grades, yet you could build a house, or a car, or something better that they couldn't dream of. What if you weren't made to balance a spread sheet but rather make beautiful furniture, or care for livestock, or write music? Society will tell you what it thinks you should do. Sadly, we're stupid enough to listen, so we take these gifts to the grave.

Dr. Monroe puts it like this: "...buried in the cemetery are books that were never written. In the cemetery are buried music that was never played. Paintings that were never painted are in the cemetery. The graveyard is filled with businesses that never opened; magazines that were never published; ideas that never became reality. Visions that never became a reality are in the cemetery. What a wealthy place. The graveyard is a rich place, because buried in the graveyard are great men who died as alcoholics; awesome women who died as prostitutes. What a wealthy place. Why? Because people took their treasure to the cemetery."

This is the punchline. If you get nothing else out of this book get this;

You're not special. You're **gifted***.*

YOU'RE TOO LOUD

My entire life, I've been told that I was loud. I come by it honest from my father, which is funny because he has been one of my biggest critics on this point (if you're reading this, I love you, old man.) But it's something that has plagued me practically from birth.

That is, until I realized it wasn't a curse; it was a gift.

I should have known I had a gift for talking much earlier than I did. I was barely able to talk when my now late grandmother used to call me her "little preacher-man." My father was a minister for a time, and in imitating him, I would line up stuffed animals and deliver speeches and sermons to them, using *Land Before Time* quotes as my scripture. At two, three, and four years old, I probably quoted the movies as well as most career preachers do the Bible. It's funny, because you know it's true.

More than once in grade school, I got into trouble for talking too much. I'd say a third of the time I had only said one or two sentences while my cohorts had been having full blown conversations, yet I'd be the one getting caught, either because my voice carries, or I had no volume control. Probably a healthy mix of both.

Favorite phrases arose among my critics: "Do you ever stop

talking?", "Do you have an inside voice?" and the simplest one, "You're so loud." As I got older, my control did get better, but the expectation also got higher and so it seemed like I was only criticized more. Eventually, I began to take it personally; like there was something wrong with me. I needed to talk less, and when I did talk, I needed to talk softly. Even then, it was probably better that I said nothing at all. The world was winning. My gift was being stifled, and I was convinced it was for my better interest. I don't hold the people who said these things at fault. Sure, they had the best of intentions (most of the time) but I also don't think they knew what they were asking. I give them the benefit of the doubt because I was twenty-four years old before I realized it myself.

SOMETHING TO SAY

It wasn't until I heard Dr. Monroe talk about the wealth of the cemetery that things clicked. This was twenty-three years into my life, and the realization didn't come to me immediately; much like a growing tree, the roots grew slowly till they finally found the nutrient-rich water. But just because the tree reaches the nutrients doesn't mean it springs to full maturity overnight; it takes time. For me, this growth took several weeks. It happened something like this:

1) I watched the video for the first time while doing leadership research to build the program.

2) I showed the Airman Leader Corp the video as I rolled out the development program.

3) I incubated the information for a few days, allowing the inspiration boil into a passion.

4) Someone reminded me yet again that I was loud.

It's worth noting that for whatever reason, this particular time stung. It stung to the point that, as a grown man, for two days I made a concerted effort to be less outspoken. It actually caused me a fair amount of depression. Other factors were playing into this at the time too, but this isn't a biography, and I promise there's a point. I'm getting there.

5) An epiphany occurred. I like to think it was the Holy Spirit being stirred in me. You can think whatever you want.

It was during this epiphany that I realized that my whole life had been building up to something. What was that something? I had no clue. At that moment though, as I ruminated over the comments given in half-jest, I realized that they were right. Everyone was right. I was loud. God had given me a voice that was nearly impossible to miss. Why? Because he gave me a message.

Do you see it yet? From birth, I've had a gift, one that God wanted me to use to speak a message into the world and the world had done everything it could to stop me. It still is. It's doing the same to you right now, and you don't even see it.

GIVE UNTO OTHERS

Give unto others, that others may give.

I built this mission statement not long after my epiphany moment. It was at the same time that I started writing my first lesson, "Don't Suck", while I was still in Technical School. You see, we're not meant to keep our gifts for ourselves. We are not placed on this earth only to satisfy our own desires. Matter of fact, if you've ever tried this, you'll realize that the more you try to satiate your desire, whatever it be, the more you crave. It's this never-ending cycle of gluttony that we fall into. Don't believe me?

In our adolescence, when we get our first taste of sugar what do we instantly do? We want more. In our childhood, when we get a new toy, or a new freedom, or, god forbid, an allowance, what do we always want? More. For those of you reading this who have had sex, when have you ever said that you wanted less sex? You don't. You never say that. You might say you don't want it anymore (or ever) from a certain person, but the fact is that you will always crave more intimate interaction. You could apply this to food, money, vacations, people in your life, trophies, Superbowl rings, Nobel Peace prizes, number one best-selling novels, whatever! The bottom line is that you will never have enough to satisfy yourself through selfish indulgence.

11

How, then, do we find fulfillment? You do it by giving, and I don't just mean your money, though charity is amazing. I mean give of yourself: give your time, your heart, your mind; sacrifice for someone, be willing to die to yourself to help someone else out and see what it does to your heart. See how it affects your soul.

True fulfillment doesn't actually come in a neatly-wrapped present box with a bow. It's not served to you at the dinner table, or on your birthday, or in your bedroom. Fulfillment requires some amount of sacrifice.

Give unto others.

Why do you do this? I could give you a Biblical answer, but those of you who are Christians already know why, and those of you who aren't probably don't care about the Bible, so I won't harp on you. Rather, I'll give you the human answer.

First, it makes us feel good. The drug released into your brain when you do something charitable is called Oxytocin. Now, this release typically doesn't happen when you give money, sorry. You'll have to find another way to get this. One that is less lazy (don't be a short-cut-taking turd). Oxytocin is great and we'll talk more about why in a bit.

Second, sacrifice is how we grow. This shouldn't come as a surprise. You might be fooling yourself thinking that somehow watching television is helping you grow. How? When was the last time watching overly-sexualized superheroes (or anti-heroes) duke it out on your 80-inch-4k-super-machine-brain-leech actually challenged you? When was the last time you left knowing something that was going to help you at work, or with the homeless guy you pass at the intersection, or the friends of the kid who committed suicide from the local high school? If you're not sacrificing your time to learn, grown, build, create, serve, and comfort, then what are you sacrificing it for?

Third, it impacts those around you, and I don't just mean the person you're intending it to impact. Remember Oxytocin, which I mentioned a few paragraphs ago? Yeah, it's responsible for this too. See, you don't just get Oxytocin from doing something nice. You get it from someone doing something nice for you, too. I'm not telling you to expect things from people; my point is that not only do you feel good when you're charitable, the person you're charitable toward feels good. You're not just serving their needs; you're serving their emotions. To take it a step farther, other people who aren't even involved will get a release of this miracle chemical just by seeing you do something for someone! It's incredible! But it will cost you the one thing in your life that you have full control to give, and every time you give it, you are guaranteed to never get it back: your time.

It's this piece here that's the key to the kingdom: when you give to others, and they feel good, and others see you doing something nice, and they feel good too, then you've now influenced your immediate ten-meter radius to go out and give unto others as well. Thus:

Give unto others, that others may give.

THE GREATEST LESSON

What if I told you that I got the entire idea for that mission not just from Dr. Monroe but also from studying history? As a matter of fact, the source material I'm pulling from for this one is from World War II.

"Whoa now, how did you get this whole 'charity' thing from one of, if not the, bloodiest war in history?"

Thanks for asking.

If I were to ask, "What is the greatest lesson that we can learn from WWII?", what would you say?

Some people would talk about the atrocities of the Holocaust and how we can never permit genocide again. Good lesson, true statement, not the greatest lesson.

Others might try to say that we must make sure no singular

individual ever gets as much power as Hitler had. I would agree with the premise, but argue that today, right now, there are men that hold more power than Hitler who aren't doing atrocious things like burning masses of people. But these people would be on the right track.

See, the greatest lesson does come from analyzing Hitler, but you must realize the stark reality that Hitler didn't gas all those people alone. Hitler wasn't flying every plane that carpet-bombed the United Kingdom. Hitler wasn't in every war room meeting, or on the front lines, or burning books, or hunting Jews. Not personally. So then why do we put all the blame and give all the infamous credit to this lunatic anyway?

Simple. It was his idea.

Which leads me to the greatest lesson we can learn from WWII:

One man can't change the world, but one idea can.

TRAGEDY TO MAJESTY

World War II and the atrocities committed under the dictatorial reign of Adolf Hitler were evil. Pure evil. Forgetting about it, or simply looking at it from a distance with disdain and disgust are bandages to a bleeding wound. They're a safety net to never let it happen again. They don't make us any better in the long run. We're not growing if we are not willing to analyze the event and humble ourselves enough to learn. Hitler's ideas were evil, but they caught like wildfire and changed the world forever.

Who's to say we can't take that principle and use it for good? *Give unto others, that others may give.* Giving already releases the Oxytocin, it's already primed biologically to spread, so let's use it. I can't change the world. This book alone won't change the world, but the idea could. All I can do is share my idea and hope that you'll share it too. Make it part of your giving, but understand it cannot be the only thing you give. The idea is infectious, but there must be substance, something that will give idea weight.

Re-enter: Your Gifts.

THE PROBLEM

"**B**ut Chad, I don't know what my gifts are. What if I don't have any?"

You have them. You know you do. They're ingrained into your soul, meshed with your biology, and solidified by your history. You're not the only person that thinks like this.

Too many of us don't know what our gifts are. We don't know because we're not trained to recognize them. Matter of fact, there has never been a time in history where anyone has been able to lay it out for us, because before the mid-to-late twentieth century, the majority of people still had to figure out how to survive.

By 'survive' I don't simply mean hold a job long enough to make money and let that money feed you. I mean really survive: make sure you wouldn't freeze in the winter, that everyone actually had food when there wasn't a supermarket to go to, or when getting there was impossible due to the winter storms.

This might sound like a fantasy to you, but the reality is so much closer than you think. I'm only two generations out of this lifestyle. My grandparents, on both my mother and father's side, had to work the soil and the coal mines, as well as hunt, in order to eat. One of my grandfathers was the oldest of seven kids when his father died. His mother was an alcoholic and they lived in a two-room hut. The siblings would sleep sideways across the bed to make everyone fit. The only heat they had was

17

from a stove-top furnace that burned in the corner, and during the harsh winter nights, they would have to plaster newspapers to the walls to keep out the wind.

It's a beautiful thing that we get to live in a time where we can actually think about our gifts without fear of starvation or freezing to death. It's a wonder that we get to stand on the shoulders of better men and women who didn't have the luxury to sit and think, then transcribe those thoughts into the book that you now hold. It's nothing short of a miracle that you get to sit in the comfort of the bookstore, coffee shop, bed or home and read this book as you sip your coffee or whiskey or tea.

I say all of this not to devalue the struggle of finding our gifts, but to illuminate the heart of appreciation we should have for those who have come before us and laid the groundwork so that we can focus on making the world better and more beautiful every day. In the grand scheme of life, put into context by the backdrop of history, the struggle of identifying our gifts seems rather trivial. Yet I would argue that discovering those gifts is more difficult than mere survival.

Why?

Because there's no formula.

Hear me out. For literally thousands, if not millions, of years, humanity has been perfecting the art of survival. How to hunt, how to farm, how to build, how to craft tools and weapons and armor; it's all been programmed into us. You don't need someone to tell you to eat when you get hungry; you just do it. If there is nothing to eat, you actively seek it out; no one has to tell you to do so. Even those weirdos like me who are out there and can seemingly go days on end without food because we just forget to eat will eventually begin to feel the effects of malnutrition and seek out some form of sustenance.

It's a sad reality, but you don't need your gift to survive. I made this obvious in the intro when I was talking about great people living and dying and no one ever knowing they were great because they took their gift to the grave. If you missed that, I hope it sinks in this time.

Our gifts are the things that make the world a better place. We need to use our gifts. Not for ourselves, but for the sake of others. The good news is that we have a better opportunity to do that than we have ever had before.

THE FORMULA

Just because a formula hasn't been found yet doesn't mean there isn't one. Just like there's more than one way to skin a cat, or reach the number four in math, I'm sure there are multiple ways to find your gifts. That being said, I'm going to share the closest thing to a 'formula' that I've found so far. It's less of an equation and more of an analysis of different perspectives; pathways of thinking that might carry you to Oz, like Dorothy on the yellow brick road. I want these questions to prompt a winding path of thought that will lead you to the epiphany of your lifetime.

Side note: This won't be fast, nor easy. You've again been warned.

Questions to the Path:
1) What do you *desire* out of your life?
2) What is a *passion* you have that you cannot shake?
3) What breaks your heart?

Oddly enough, these same questions will resurface later when we talk about values, because finding our gifts directly correlates with what we value most in this life.

DESIRE

What do you desire out of life?

Most people would say that this is the easiest question to answer in the world. "I want a good job, I want a lot of money, I want a nice car, I want to be happy, I want, I want, I want…."

I don't care what you want. 'Wants' and 'desires' are very different, and the faster you learn the difference, the quicker you will be able to get something really useful out of this question.

'Wants' are fleeting. They come and go like a stiff autumn wind. Here, let me show you. I'll use a typical Tuesday morning as an example. This Tuesday morning, I woke up and I wanted more sleep. After I got up, I wanted coffee. After coffee, I wanted breakfast. After breakfast, I wanted a shower.

Need I keep going? Didn't think so.

Compare that, however, with what I desire. I desire to be closer to God, so I read my Bible and use the lessons within to help me serve. I desire to make an impact in this world, to influence people to stop squandering their gifts and instead give them back, so I'm writing this book and speaking publicly and praying that the message clicks with someone. I desire to raise a godly family, so I've changed my habits from being an adulterous porn addict to preserving what little bit of purity I have left for my future wife so that I might be an example to my children.

There should be a difference in depth when you compare 'wants' with 'desires'.

Here's another way to differentiate between the two: both 'wants' and 'desires' inspire some type of action, but who does that action serve? Every 'want' I talked about before on that typical Tuesday served only one person: Me. But every 'desire' that I talked about would somehow have a profound impact on *someone else*.

Because it's not about you. Because you're not special.

So. What do you truly desire?

PASSION

The Latin root of passion is 'patio', which literally means 'to suffer'. Now, I don't know about you, but when I think about something that I'm passionate about, the last thing I typically think of is pain. Matter of fact, I usually jump to something more akin to desire: something that I can't get my mind off of, that I keep coming back to; the things I can't help but work on; the things that I can't keep myself from talking about. My soapboxes.

Turns out, the more I thought about this, the more I realized that the things I'm really passionate about are things I would be willing to, here it is, *suffer* for.

Imagine you're in love. Some of you won't have to imagine, because you are in love, but for those of us that are single here, let's break out the dream-machine and take a trip to that place where we all hope to one day be. Imagine the person you're in love with: see their face and their smile, and imagine their comforting smell as you hold them in your arms after a long day or a significant amount of time spent away. Feel their hand in yours, gripping tight like they'll never let you go. Think of all the dreams they have, all the things they want to accomplish in their life that you want to help and support them in.

Now, imagine all of that is threatened. Doesn't matter by what. Could be another person, an illness, the direction of your life, the distance between your respective dwellings (hint: long distance sucks). You're madly, rapturously in love with this person. *Passionately* in love with them. Is there any amount of suffering you wouldn't go through for them? Is there any trial you wouldn't face down to make sure you preserved the joy and safety of the person you've imagined?

If your answer is 'yes', and you wouldn't deal with that kind of pain, then we have some different work we need to do with you.

If your answer is 'no', congratulations. You've discovered what real passion is. It is a love for something so deep that you would be willing to physically or emotionally suffer for it.

What does this have to do with gifts? Put plainly, if you have something in your life that you love so much that it hurts, you're probably not far off from finding your gift. If there is something you love to do so much that you can't imagine your life without it, figure out how you can use that passion to benefit someone else and you'll have found your gift, or come pretty dang close.

But passion isn't the only pain that will lead you to your gifts.

HEARTBREAKER

"What breaks your heart?"
- Andy Stanley

Andy did an entire sermon series on this one question, and if you want more of a Biblical perspective, I highly recommend looking it up. What we need here is an analysis of why this helps us discover our gifts.

Let's get something straight first. If a girlfriend, boyfriend, whoever, breaks your heart that does not mean that they were your gift. If that's where your brain took this, then I think you're reading the wrong book. I'm not here to offer relationship advice, and I sure as all get-out ain't inspiring some creeper, stalker stuff.

What this means is when we look at the world, we should see problems. If we don't, we're walking blind through a fallen and dangerous world. Actual blind people have more sight than us if that's what we try to believe, trust me. I used to be that guy who could only see the good in people and I've paid for it dearly in time, money, and heartache.

Out of the problems you see in the world, most will allow you to just click right along. World hunger might not bother you. Poverty in your city might not bother you. Death rates of cancer patients might not bother you. All these things are tragic, and I'm not saying that you don't recognize them, because you do. Just like I do. They're horrible, but they don't truly break your heart. I know this because the thing that really breaks your heart, you will not be able to ignore. You'll see it and become passionate about it. If you ignore it, a feeling of disease will eat away at your insides. You'll suffer, and the suffering will continue till you choose to do something about it.

Caring about something that deeply is a gift. It's a gift that leads you to more gifts. The solution you come up with for the problem that breaks your heart will be unique to you. You have been specially equipped to deal with a problem in this world, a problem you will inevitably be passionate about solving.

THE VECTOR MODEL

In the Air Force, we have different organizational units, and each of those organizational units has its own commander and a staff below them, which eventually leads down to lowest ranked enlisted individual; namely, me. This is how we get our Chain-of-Command and I was lucky enough to have a pretty stellar chain at my first unit. My supervisors were great and their supervisor was awesome too, but the person I want to highlight was our Flight Commander. For the sake of his privacy we'll call him Bojack.

First Lieutenant Bojack, a Captain-select at the time, was one of the best leaders I had ever served under. He had a healthy (at times aggressive) competitive spirit, a mind for innovation, and charisma that could stop a freight hauler. His dashing debonair smile and thick dark hair gave him the textbook look of a 21st-century American Officer if there ever was one.

All of this was good, but what made him a great leader was that he actually cared about his people. He embodied the traits of leadership I had read about in the book 'The Mission, the Men, and Me' just before shipping off to basic training. Within his first three days of getting to the unit (he was technically my second flight commander at this unit), he pulled our flight into a room and gave a brief introduction, then opened his door to us, saying something to the effect of, "I have a real passion for helping people reach their goals. So if there is anything I can do to help you reach yours, talk to me. Let's sit down and have a conversation."

It took me less than twenty-four hours to have the man one-on-one, Mano-a-Mano, in that same conference room, saying, "I don't know what you can do to help me, but these are my passions and goals."

Lt. Bojack didn't have some crazy breakthrough idea for me in that moment, but what he shared has stuck with me and bloomed into the principles you're about to learn.

Bojack called this idea 'having a wide vector'.

I call it 'The Vector Model'.

TOO MANY OPTIONS

Lt. Bojack might have given me the breakthrough principle, but the seeds of this idea were planted just a few weeks after my arrival to the since-deactivated Detachment 4, which was a month or more before the arrival of Bojack himself.

On a crowded development floor, trying to complete training and actually be useful to my unit, and figure out what I wanted to do with this gift for public speaking that I felt called by God to use, I found myself, my supervisor, and a contractor named Soto in tears.

We were laughing. Laughing at me.

Well, we were really laughing at my supervisor's goofy attitude, which in this particular case was prompted by me not being able to figure out what in the holy heck I wanted to do with myself. Over the past week I had sought help with degree plans, certifications, Officer Training School packages, Senior Airman Below the Zone packages, unit transfer requests, potentially becoming a chaplain, and God knows what else. It got to the point where my Puerto Rican supervisor, in one of his goofy voices (one that sounded somewhere between a Brooklyn, NY, accent and broken English) said, "Ya know your problem? Ya got too many options!" Complete with knife-hand and all.

This became a running joke that I'm sure would register even now, but what made it so funny wasn't the weird voice, or the mannerisms. It was the fact that it was 100% true. Without a doubt, I simply had too many options.

As we grow up, we develop interests. As we spend time and effort on these interests, we discover what we really enjoy, what we only kind of enjoy for a time, and what we actually don't enjoy at all. As we grow some more, we gain maturity and those interests mature with us. A love of reading develops into a love of writing. Singing in the car leads us to being a music minor in college and serving on the worship team at church. Riding bikes leads to racing cars or becoming a mechanic.

The directions of our lives are set at a very young age, but it's not until we grow and mature that we are able to look back and see exactly how one thing led to another.

Kind of.

See, I was that guy who was good at whatever I set my mind to, and I tended to set my mind on *a lot* of things. It started with football for fourteen years, which ended in a year playing division one for Marshall University. I got into mechanical stuff because of my senior year physics class which led to me trying engineering in college for a semester. (Hint: It only lasted a semester.) I worked in construction multiple times in my life, with my dad while growing up (he was a painting contractor in those days and did some drywall work too) and in my early adulthood. I managed a lifeguard team at a local pool over a summer. I was a ballroom dance instructor, and eventually became a majority owner in a small studio in Buford, Ga, before going to work at Medieval Times as a Squire when my own business didn't work out. I thought about doing real-estate because I really was good at selling things, but decided on taking the military path while I was still young, hoping to make it down range as a Tactical Air Control Party member and blow some stuff up. I grew up reading and writing and started writing my first novel (which I finished but have yet to publish as of this writing) when I was 18. I did some DJing in and after college. I loved, and still love, learning about history and the meta-narrative of our world.

All of that and I ended up with an IT job in the Air Force somehow.

I saw success in all those things to a degree, yet none of them got me any closer to living what I felt was a fulfilled or valuable life. My interests, and my life, were like spokes on a wheel and I was the hub. None of them correlated.

Until I made them correlate.

FINDING A VECTOR

In physics, a 'Vector' is defined as a value (a number, or a thing, anything) that has both magnitude and direction. We usually represent a vector with a line that has an arrow at one end showing in which direction the thing is moving.

You're probably thinking, "That's super nerdy! Why do I care?"

The answer is simple. The trajectory of your life can be modeled with a vector the same way force or statistics can be. Matter of fact, the Vector Model tends to describe several of our basic human desires better than the psychology books I read in college.

How? Simple really. What are two of the most common things people want out of life?

1) They want to feel like they're making an impact.

Well that's magnitude. Literally, the measure of how large your impact is.

2) They want to feel like they have a purpose. In other words, they're working toward ………………….something.

That's direction. It's where your life is going, what it's leading up to.

Your vector doesn't have to be a single line, though. As a matter of fact, I would advise explicitly against getting too specific with your 'destination'. The only real destination any of us will reach is death. Till you get close to that point, keep your vector wide. That's what Bojack would say.

What does having a wide vector mean? And how does all of this relate back to finding our gifts and where to utilize them?

Keep reading. I have pictures coming to help.

JUST THROW THE BALL

In baseball, or softball, the Pitcher has a designated strike zone. Their entire goal is to get the ball that is in their hand into that strike zone, without letting the batter hit the ball. After taking a breath and deciding what type of pitch they want to throw, the Pitcher winds up, accelerates their arm, and releases the ball.

At this point, the pitcher is at the mercy of fate. They've sent the ball in a direction, with a certain speed (magnitude), creating a vector with each and every pitch.

Football players do it, too. A Quarterback calls a play, gets his team lined up, and gives the signal for the center to snap the ball. He steps back, makes his checks down field to find the best receiving target, rears back his arm, and lets it fly. The ball sails through the air on a vector toward a receiver with the ultimate intention of getting across the goal line.

In both of these scenarios, the player (Pitcher or Quarterback) has control of deciding in which direction to send the ball, and how much velocity to send it with. Magnitude and direction.

You have the same control over your life. You're the Quarterback. You're the Pitcher. The difference is you don't just have one ball to send down field. You have a near-endless supply of interests scattered about you like ammunition waiting to be loaded into the gun called ambition and fired down range toward your goals. However, before you can load your interests, you have to collect them, you have to get them moving in the same direction.

Imagine you're the hub of a wheel: Each interest you have juts off of that hub like the spokes of a wheel. If you're anything like me, some of those spokes are longer than others, some are curved, and none of them are working together. They're all haphazardly strewn around you in some funky amalgamation that you have no clue what to do with. Kinda like this;

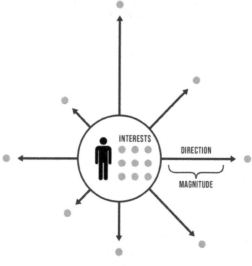

This is your life, and your interests, without the Vector Model. None of them are working toward a goal (direction), and since all of your time is scattered, you're losing a lot of your motivation and energy, which means you feel like you're not making an impact (magnitude).

What if we changed that? What if we were able to find a way to tie those interests together and direct them to a common direction? Not a destination! Just a direction. What would things look like then?

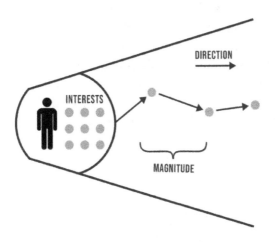

Boom. Now instead of having all of your time spread between multiple different areas and getting nowhere, everything you do, pleasure or work, leads you in a desired direction.

Now why do I say avoid setting a destination? Let's go back to the sports analogy.

After the ball leaves the player's hand, does that player have any more control over that ball? No. It's up to fate for that ball to reach the player's desired location. Want to know a secret? It typically never does. It gets close to be sure! And sometimes, the player will luck out and get a perfect strike or throw a perfect pass, but typically, the ball varies just slightly off of the intended destination. The outcome could be the exact same as what was originally desired: touchdowns, strikes, outs. Or it could be vastly different: interceptions, balls, walks.

The thing about life is that you don't know what God, or the universe, or fate have planned for you. You just don't. You need a general direction, complete with a preferred outcome, but avoid ultimatums; this keeps you from pigeon-holing yourself. Keep your vector wide; account for the unpredictability of life now, so you're prepared for it when it occurs.

Like I said before, the ultimate destination is death. For all of us. Make sure you're maximizing your impact (magnitude) while you still have a chance. Don't get bogged down with wondering how close you'll get to the target, and don't fret about whether or not your ultimatum will be achieved. Instead, know what direction you're heading, what it is you want to work toward, what your passion and desires are, what breaks your heart, then rear back and throw the damn ball.

God—or fate—will handle the rest.

THE "ITS" METHOD

The ITS method I'm about to share with you is a moral and ethical way of getting ahead in life. We talk later about the necessity of getting ahead and jumping the gun, but I feel it is imperative to share this principle now because it can directly help you with your vectoring. In essence, this method is a decision-making thought process that allows you to analyze a situation, assume various outcomes based on the moving parts you can see, then plot a course of action through that situation. The best part of the ITS method is that it also provides room for flexibility. Since you'll be thinking through the variables of a situation, it will allow you have a prepared response for when things don't go how you think they will (which they rarely do).

Let's start by defining the acronym: ITS stands for "If", "Then", "So". A more specific breakdown of the method looks like this;

If these are my variables;
Then these are the possible outcomes;
So, my next course of action should be;

Pretty simple right? It's supposed to be. Decision making is hard enough as it is; we shouldn't over complicate it more than necessary, and hopefully this method will help to simplify it even further. Since I'm not special and this came from my brain, then there's nothing particularly special about it other than it's effective. And since you're not special either, this method should work for you just as well as it works for me. The only two things this method requires is critical thinking and a bit of imagination. Used effectively, it will help you maximize your efforts when getting good, using your gifts, and jumping the gun.

As we move through the explanation of the method, I'm going to illustrate its use by giving a simple example of its application in my own life. The context for this example goes like this: I had a friend who was in love with a girl who was moving to the other side of the country. They didn't know how things were going to work, but they wanted to try. This is where I stepped in with the ITS method to break down the possible outcomes.

IF

"If these are my variables…"

In order to get to this question, there is actually a prerequisite question that logic calls us to ask, which is, "What are my variables?"

Now I don't recommend writing these down unless you're in a super complex situation and trying to make sense of things. Most of the situations I use the ITS method for are simple enough where I don't need to write down the variables, and even for the more complex situations, I refrain from writing down the variables because this can actually over-complicate the problem. The goal is to keep things simple, and if you force yourself to work with the main details that you can remember, you'll do a better job at simplifying the problem because only the biggest variables will stick out.

Once you have the big variables in mind, you need to sort them a bit. Not every variable is going to combine with the other variables.

In the example of my friend, the variables were something like this;

1) His feelings for her.

2) Her feelings for him.

3) Her feelings about the other people in the same town/area as him.

4) His feelings about the people and area in the place she was moving to.

5) His Career.

6) Her Career.

Now, the first step is figuring out which of these variables actually matter and fit together. Because I had first-hand experience with both my friend and his girlfriend (she was a close friend as well, even before they were dating) and their feelings for each other, I could say with confidence that they wouldn't let their careers get in the way of them being together. That automatically narrowed the variable selection by a third.

Our current viable pool now looks like this:

1) His feelings for her.

2) Her feelings for him.

3) Her feelings about the other people in the same town/area as him.

4) His feelings about the people and area in the place she was moving to.

This doesn't get us far, but it's what we need for a starting point.

THEN

"Then my possible outcome is…"

Okay, I changed it a bit from the opening section. You'll understand why in a second.

This part of the method applies a bit of that critical thinking and imagination I was talking about. You need both the logic and creativity if you're going to get a realistic outcome to carry into the next segment.

In the "then" segment, you analyze the variables and create potential outcomes from the possibilities. Some of the outcomes are going to be out of your control. Those things you have to offer up to God, or chance, or fate, or whatever, and focus on the things you can control, but have a contingency for what your actions will be if something you cannot control changes.

Let's take a look at our example to get a clearer picture. Our current variable pool has four parts.

1) His feelings for her.

2) Her feelings for him.

3) Her feelings about the other people in the same town/area as him.

4) His feelings about the people and area in the place she was moving to.

The next step is to make actual If/Then statements with the variables at play.

1) If his feelings about her change, then they'll break up.

2) If her feelings about him change, then they'll break up.

Boom. First two done, and those ultimatums happen regardless of what other variables are at play. Powerful variables like these make things super simple. Let's look at the next set and see how things work out.

3) If his feelings for her don't change and he likes the people and the area she is moving to, it is likely he will move to be with her.

4) If her feelings for him don't change and she misses the "family" that she made in the time she was living in the same area as him, it is likely she will return.

Get the gist? You could take the equation the other way too, and ask, "what if she feels the same for him but doesn't miss the area?" and the same for him. The answer is, one of them moves to be with the other, or it strains their relationship to the point that their feelings change and the outcomes of the first scenarios come true. Essentially, this whole system comes down to logical role-playing in your brain based on factual evidence.

But why do we go through the process of asking these questions and building out these scenarios?

That's where the "So" part comes in.

SO

"So, my course of action should be…"

The whole purpose of the first two steps is to build scenarios. We build scenarios in order to plot a course of action. The course of action is made in order to achieve a desired outcome, or to avoid an undesirable one. This should be pretty self-evident. Building scenarios also allows us to have a contingency. Should things not go your way, you're more prepared to make a choice on the next course of action based on the planning you've already accomplished by using the ITS method.

You might be thinking, "Well what course of action could

you have taken in another person's relationship," in relation to our example scenario.

The answer is: None.

But I helped lay things out in a more readable fashion for my friend.

For instance:

2) If her feelings about him change, then they'll break up. So, in order to avoid her having a change of heart about him, he should be patient and kind and understanding with their long-distance situation and make it as easy on her as he can.

In the event of the success of scenario two, scenario four comes into play:

4) If her feelings for him don't change and she misses the "family" that she made in the time she was living in the same area as him, it is likely she will return. So, in order to make her move back to his town easier, he should visit her family and gain their blessing, letting her know that she won't be isolated from them by choosing him, and prepare a place for her in his life as best he can to make the transition easier.

Now, in reality, I never laid out the "So" part for my friend. He's smart enough to figure that part out on his own. For the sake of transparency, I don't think my sharing of the scenarios I built around this relationship influenced his actions in the slightest. I believe that God meant for him and his girlfriend to be together and there was nothing I could have said to change that.

My scenarios ended up being dead accurate, though. She moved away, spent three months away from him, realized he was her home now, found a job, and moved back to be with him. Having friends who were basically family in the area made the choice easier, but at the end of the day, she did it all to be with him. He helped make it happen by making the distance on her as easy as possible and helping to prepare a place for her in his life for when she got back. They're slated to be married in 94 days, as of this writing.

If that doesn't make your heart feel good, I don't know what will. The reason I chose this scenario was because it's a feel-good story, and because it shows the accuracy and validity of the ITS method.

Don't be fooled by the lack of "do or die" in the example. Just because people's lives, or millions of dollars, or someone's career wasn't on the line doesn't mean that this method can't help you in those areas either. It helps with jumping the gun on the coward because, done properly, it will give you an accurate depiction of what's on the line if you let it win, and you'll have a better idea of when to expect it to show up.

I use this method so often that it happens subconsciously for me now. I build scenarios and play them out constantly with everything, especially the important stuff, because it gets me prepared for what I'm about to face and for how I can best use my gifts. Nothing makes me special. If I can do it, you can too.

THE PITFALL

There is one pitfall to the ITS method that I need to make you aware of. I learned of this pitfall by reading "The Screwtape Letters" by great academic and author C.S. Lewis. The passage that illuminated this pitfall to me is as follows:

"What you must do is to keep running in his mind (side by side with the conscious intention of doing his duty) the vague idea of all sorts of things he can do or not do, *inside* the framework of the duty, which seem to make him a little safer. Get his mind off the simple rule ('I've got to stay here and do so-and-so') into a series of imaginary life lines ('If A happened - though I very much hope it won't - I could do B - and if the worst came to the worst, I could always do C')... The point is to keep him feeling that he has *something*, other than the Enemy and courage the supplies, *to fall back on*, so that what was intended to be a total commitment to duty becomes honeycombed all through with little unconscious reservations."

What Lewis means by this in context of the ITS method (which is almost perfectly paraphrased in the excerpt above) is that we cannot become so concerned with projecting the future outcomes that we forget to do our duty and *act* in the moment. Your actions in the present moment mean more than any projecting you could do. The only reason you are using the ITS method to project at all is to better understand how to act in the present. For this reason, I will reiterate my point from the beginning of this chapter and remind you to *keep the scenarios overly simple*. The better you can reduce the situation to a binary choice, the more quickly you can deduce your actions in the moment so that you may put them to practice. Your goal is to act, not to project every possibility forever. Keep it simple; project only what you must; then act.

Remember this: A bad plan executed well is better than a great plan executed poorly. Often, the best course of action is to simply *take action*.

GIT GUD

If you know anything about me, you know I'm a fan of video games. Though I condemned them earlier because they were responsible for a large part of the road blocks I encountered in my teens and early adulthood, and still today threaten to occupy precious time that is far better spent doing something productive, they still hold a very special place in my heart. Every now and then I'll sit down to "relax" and play a game for an hour or so and revel in the glories of modern technology.

I put "relax" in quotations like that because most people would see the level of skill, and oftentimes frustration, that it takes to play the games that I really enjoy and say, "No thanks. Those are too hard." Not only are they hard, they tend to be frustrating to the point of wanting to throw something. This is why you typically see a stress ball next to my console. Not because I squeeze it, but because it gives me something to throw that is far less likely to break anything.

Why subject myself to something like this? Because the payoff of success feels so much better when the skill cap is high. If the game doesn't have a decent skill cap, it better have one heck of a story or I'll get two hours in and set it down, never to come back. I just don't have the patience for something that's going to waste my time.

For all you nay-sayers out there that say hard games aren't worth it (you know the games I'm talking about; Sekiro, Dark

Souls, First-Person Shooters, Cuphead, etc.) I only have two words for you.

Git Gud.

For those of you who are completely lost right now because games aren't your thing, "Git Gud" (pronounced the same as 'Get good' because the 21st century culture is dumb) is a phrase those who are in the elite category of gamers say to the casuals who don't want to put in the time to be good at something but are more than willing to complain about it. In other words, it's how we stir the pot and get a rise out of people. Super Christian thing to do? Probably not, but we all have flaws and this one is too much fun because the only people who actually get upset by it take themselves way too seriously. If that's you, chill, bro. It's a game.

What does any of this have to do with gifts, vectors, values and beliefs? Everything actually. "Git Gud" is what I've named this set of principles because there is literally no harder game than the game of life and the only way you'll ever be successful at using your gifts is if you hone them one step at a time. In other words, you've got to "Git Gud".

Matter of fact, this principle can be dated back as early as the first and second century to a guy named Petrus who was traveling around the middle east. Petrus' name literally translates to "rock", so from here in I'm going to refer to him as The Rock (not Dwayne Johnson, the original Rock) because it sounds cool. Forgive my self-indulgence.

Now, the Rock was a theologian who wrote a few letters to some colleagues while on his travels, one of which lays out the following principle:

"…make every effort to add to your faith goodness; and to goodness, knowledge; and to knowledge, self-control; and to self-control, perseverance; and to perseverance, godliness; and to godliness, mutual affection; and to mutual affection, love."

To the Rock, there was nothing more important than faith.

I tend to agree with him; feel free to disagree with us, but the principle still stands. From my perspective, if this equation was strong enough to be the key to the most important thing in The Rock's life, and also my own, why wouldn't it work for things that are far easier and less significant? And if faith isn't important to you, you can just swap out that word for whatever you value the most and I guarantee that this will still work. Old dudes like The Rock tend to have a knack for that sort of thing.

You might be wondering, "What equation? This has nothing to do with math." Well, neither did the Vector Model, but it still works.

The thing is, if you want to get good at something, what you really have to do is start at the bottom rung of this ladder and work your way up. Back to front. Last to first. No skipping steps. No cheating the system. You want to "Git Gud"? The formula is right here, and I'm going to help you break it down.

It all starts with Love.

LOVE

How do you know that you love something? Truly love it? Well, I hate to burst most of your bubbles but it ain't a feeling. Matter of fact, it's the exact inverse of a feeling. Love is a choice. It has to be, because typically the things we love are the things that cause us the most pain.

Remember how we were talking about passion? How the Latin root of that word is 'patio' which means 'to suffer' and how the things we're passionate about are things we're willing to suffer for? Yeah. Same thing with love. Matter of fact, Simon Sinek is fond of saying that "Passion isn't an input, it's an output." In other words, it's not the starting place, it's the result.

Imagine for a moment that money wasn't an issue. You

could do anything you wanted in life and money, or the lack thereof, would never be a barrier to you. What would you do? Don't just glaze over this and keep reading. In your mind, I want you to pretend you are talking to me right now and say, "Chad, I would…" and finish the sentence. Imagine I took that thing away from you. Whether it's writing, or raising children, serving your community, playing basketball or video games or music, it's gone! I just took it away! What do you feel? Is it pain? An emotional hurt in your chest that aches? If not, then you need to choose a different answer to my original question. If you are hurting, can you tell me why? Some of you might answer me with, "It's what I'm passionate about," but I think we get this wrong. We get it wrong for the same reason that Simon Sinek points out to us. Passion isn't an input. It's not a catalyst. What you feel in your chest when I take that thing from you, that's proof that you are passionate about that thing, but that passion has a source. Take the phrase, "I _____ (something)." This could be:

I enjoy hiking.

I hate cruelty.

I dislike people.

I like food.

Now try the same thing, but swap out the verbs with the word "passion":

I passion hiking.

I passion cruelty.

I passion people.

I passion food.

It doesn't make sense and it's not just because I'm playing with syntax. It doesn't make sense because passion is a feeling, not an action. It's what you get out after adding something else in. Since we've established that passion, this pain that that spurns us to take action for a variety of reasons, is a result of something; what is it the result of? In life the answer is "many things". When we're talking about our scenario from before, and especially when getting good at our gifts, the answer is much simpler: *Love*.

I have never once been passionate about something that I did not love, and if you take time to really analyze your own life, I'm sure that you would find a similar trend because it's simply not possible. Why would you be willing to suffer for something that you don't love? Seems like a stupid question, because there are people in the corporate and government structure who feel as though they suffer every day for something that they don't love, but if you asked them if they are passionate about that thing, they would also inevitably tell you, "No."

You can experience pain from a situation without love, but you'll never experience passion without it.

Why does all of this matter? Because love is the catalyst. If you want to 'Git Gud' at something you're going to have to love it first. There's no way around it. You'll never find an NBA Basketball player who didn't love basketball before they got good at it. You'll never find a successful neurosurgeon who didn't somehow fall in love with the sciences before they got good at being a doctor. You'll never find a famous musician who didn't first fall in love with music, or a successful dancer who didn't fall in love with movement, or a professional gamer who didn't first fall in love with video games. It just doesn't happen.

This is hard for most people because most people are afraid to commit. This keeps people from truly experiencing what it means to love something. They miss out on the greatest part of life because of the vulnerability that comes with loving something. I hate to tell you, but if this is you, get over it. Face the fear of being hurt, face the fear of being let down, face the fear of failure, and commit to loving something. If you don't, you'll end up being one of those people who needs a tombstone. You don't want to be a person who needs a tombstone. Live a life worthy of not needing a tombstone. Live a life full of love. Your gifts, and your ability to use them to their fullest, starts with your innate capacity to love.

MUTUAL AFFECTION

Alrighty! You've made up your mind to commit. You've Vectored your life and know what direction you want to move in, you know your desires, your passions, what breaks your heart, and what you love to do. Great! New secret reveal. Your choice to love that thing and commit to it will never be enough.

You need a team. A team that will hold you accountable, and a team that will fill your blind spots. Let's face it, we all suck at being our own accountability partners. It's a fact. Why? Because we know ourselves better than anyone else does, which makes it super easy for us to build the most convincing arguments that justify why it's okay to go back on what we've committed to.

The twelve steps of Alcoholics Anonymous says that you can master the first eleven steps perfectly, but if you fail at mastering the twelfth step, you are destined to relapse. That last step? Help another recovering alcoholic. This is important, because it is a prime example of accountability. By helping someone else, they now have a standard that they have shared with another person. They've become both a role model and mentor. In most cases, it's easy to let ourselves down, let slip our resolve, relapse into that thing that could ruin our lives. It's a lot harder to do that when you think about how you would explain your relapse to someone looking up to you, or an accountability partner whose opinion you highly value.

You gifts, loves, and commitments work the exact same way. If you don't have other people in your life to help hold you accountable, you'll never make it. You'll let yourself get away with anything. Other people who care about you and are invested in you will not let you falter. Even if they never say anything to you, if you care enough about them to share your loves and passions with them, you'll want to uphold those things even more for fear of disappointing them.

The podcasts, the public speaking events, my education, and this book; none of it would have gotten done were it not for the team of people God placed around me. I'm not going to beat around the faith bush on this one. The only reason you're reading this right now is because God put a team of people in my life exactly when they needed to be there, exactly where they needed to be in order for this to get finished. Every time I sought out people on my own to build my team, because I knew I needed a team, I failed. Miserably. Either the people weren't interested, or they weren't actually someone that I wanted to be a part of the vision. Regardless, they weren't the right people. The right people have always come along by what most people (even some Christians) would call coincidence. I call it God, and you'll never change my mind.

This team is so significant because without them, the book wouldn't have been edited. The podcasts would sound like crap. The content we produce wouldn't be half as good as what it is. The lives we're touching wouldn't be growing the way they are. None of it is possible without the team, because they fill my blind spots and bring to the table gifts of their own. Gifts that allow them to accomplish things I would never be able to, that make me better every single day. The team isn't possible without mutual affection, and mutual affection isn't possible without love.

Yup. I went there. You're not going to develop mutual affection unless you're willing to love someone else. You must open your heart, be willing to serve other people, and be willing to love them. This doesn't have to be super intimate. Matter of fact, I would reserve the super intimate love for only those closest to you—your significant other and your dearest friends. But that doesn't keep you from loving and serving the other people on your team.

We'll talk more in a later chapter about building teams or learning to be a part of an existing team. For now, understand accountability and filling your blind spots.

Accountability keeps you honest.

Filling your blind spots will make you, and the people on your team, stronger and more powerful than the sum of your parts.

Reminder: None of this means a freaking thing if you fail to keep love at the center of it all - love not only for what you do, but love for the people around you as well.

GODLINESS

This one is going to be hard for some of you to swallow, but here's the bottom line: this whole formula hinges on this one point. You miss this, you miss what The Rock was trying to teach us. So even if you don't believe in a god, pay attention.

I have spent weeks researching Godliness, trying to find the best way to present this to a secular audience. It's been both riveting and immensely complex... I've read so much and studied so much on the topic of Godliness now I could write my own thesis. I saved you the trouble of all that, and rather than going into a full apologetics argument (which would be a book of its own) I'm going to try to give you the highlights.

Godliness, in the simplest definition, means to adhere to the commands and/or rules of God. For those who believe in God (Christian, Jew, Muslim, Mormon, etc.), you should be well acquainted with the premise, though you may be struggling with practice. Nevertheless, the commands and guidelines are best surmised in one word: Law. It's what we abide by, or are supposed to abide by, and in doing so, we exhibit Godliness.

But what if you don't believe in God? Does that exempt you from this part of the process? Do you get to skip this step of getting good?

No. Why?

Because even if you want to argue that there is no God, what you can't argue (at least not without contradicting your other perceived values) is that there is no natural law. By natural law, I mean a law of right and wrong, good and evil that is programmed into nature itself. This natural law is what gives us human rights, it's the foundation of our constitution here in the United States and it's the reason why western culture has progressed past such barbaric institutions as slavery and the oppression of women.

More specific examples would be something like this: I'm in my back yard and littered around me are the dismembered parts of several kittens. My hands are covered in their blood, the knife is still in my hand, and I have this amazingly satisfied look on my face. My neighbor sees from their porch. What do you think her reaction should be? The answer is to call the cops and put me in prison for animal cruelty. Though a human law exists for that, you don't need one to know that slaughtering innocent, helpless kittens is wrong. It doesn't matter that I'm a well-off, white, religious male who works in the entertainment industry and was abused as a child (I wasn't by the way). It also doesn't matter if the neighbor who saw me was a Black-American doctor who grew up in the Bronx and converted to Islam and married an immigrant from Bali. *Literally none of that matters!* The only thing that matters in this equation is that one person saw another person doing something that violated the natural law and knew in their gut that it was wrong.

So without the fluff, let's answer the question;

What is Universal Godliness? What is a Godliness that all people can subscribe to?

Godliness, in the context that we are covering here, is adherence and obedience to a moral and ethical law. Read that again. And again. And again.

If you cannot hold yourself to a moral and ethical standard, this formula will not work for you. If you cannot agree to live your life by the moral and ethical standards of the natural law of the world, then you cannot hope to gain success using the formula The Rock has given us.

But now that we've established what Godliness means, and I've made it clear that the rest of the formula hinges on it, let's talk about the *why*.

This level of devotion and obedience to a law that is higher than yourself provides humility and acceptance to unknown variables in your life. It also gives direction in times of doubt. Most importantly, it should help with setting a direction that is not only beneficial to you, but to those around you as well.

These are broad ideas on purpose. Many scholars have written many books on the subject of Godliness and I could write one myself, but that is not the topic of this book. My only goal here is to give you basic understanding.

I also don't expect you to believe that natural law comes without complications. Life is not black and white; there is a ton of grey areas. This does not diminish the necessity of the natural law, your obedience to it, your Godliness. Actually, it enhances the necessity. Having a clear perspective of the natural law to which you adhere will gift you clarity when the options seem grey and hazy.

Lastly, your mutual affection is imperative to your Godliness. You are not special, and you are definitely not perfect. The sooner you humble yourself to this fact, the sooner you can learn how to handle the disappointment that comes when you fail yourself. Those around you, those to whom you give mutual affection, and those closest from whom you receive it, should have a similar view of Godliness. Because you are going to fail in your obedience. But having a community to hold you accountable, and to get you back on track when you fall short of the mark is quintessential to getting good.

Collectively, with love for something, mutual affection and support from your community, and the ability to obey and adhere to a moral and ethical standard, you are now equipped to persevere.

PERSEVERANCE

The hardest challenges you will ever face in your life are mental. I know this because I have lived it. I've crawled and rolled and drug my face through sewage run-off. I've walked a mile through forty-degree lightning storms with rain coming at me sideways with a hundred pounds on my back. I've walked five miles through pitch black woods without a flashlight, same hundred-pound backpack on, looking for what amounted to a mile marker just so I could make it back to camp and get a few extra minutes of sleep that night. The hardest part of all of it was the mental decision that I wouldn't quit.

Some of you who are reading this are probably thinking that you'd have to be insane to undergo some of the things I described above. I assure you, there are people who have gone through worse. My brother is one of them. My former teammates are others. But measuring your challenges against mine is not the point of this. I gave you that piece because I wanted to illustrate my experience, not devalue your own, and the point remains: the hardest challenges you will ever face are mental.

Think back on your life and you'll find the truth of that statement in your own history. Were you a high school or college athlete? Then you know that just waking up and getting to practice was often the hardest part of playing that sport. What about a college student? How many classes did you have at 8:00am that you had to force yourself out of bed for, or how many all-nighters did you pull in the library just trying to finish that thesis?

What's the hardest thing you've ever done in your life to this point? How did you do it? Was it the actions? Or was it the aspect of deciding you wouldn't fail, you wouldn't give up, you wouldn't take no for an answer?

This is perseverance.

My mother has to be one of the strongest women I have ever met. She might be mad at me for sharing something with you, but I can think of no better example of a person who has persevered in their life.

You see, there are two specific instances in her life that scream perseverance to me like no other. More than my introductory line of crap, and more than I have seen from almost anyone besides maybe my brother, whose story I don't feel comfortable sharing.

The first demonstration of perseverance my mother exhibited she had help with, which comes back to that mutual affection thing I was talking about before. See, mom has had three children. Only two of us are alive today. That's because my sister, the eldest of us, was born with a complication in her chromosomes that usually ends in a miscarriage or still-born child. My sister, however, lived for five months after her birth. If ever there was a person worthy of the surname Garrett, one of the meanings of which is 'Warrior', it was her.

My mother, newlywed and still just a kid by most people's view, watched over her and cared for her as she watched her baby struggle for life and then fade away. The burden she must have felt I can only imagine. The pain that came in the years I could not begin to imagine, and I pray to never experience what she and my father must have gone through. It took years, but my dad finally begged my mother enough that she gave in, and they tried again for a second child, my older brother. To persevere through the pain of losing one child, and the fear that you might lose another, hoping and praying every day that you don't have to relive the horror of watching your child waste away before your eyes… It's a fate I would wish on no one. Yet my mother pushed through.

But her troubles did not stop there. Sadly, there are other battles in life that we all must face. Fear, anxiety, and depression chase us all. I use that would specifically because of how my mother has told me this story, a story that has a timeline that I believe continues to this very day.

After having my brother and giving him some time to grow, my mother went back to school. She graduated with honors and went on to work in accounting at some of the largest corporations in the world, Bank of America being the largest. At one point in her career, she was even given the opportunity to become an executive for her division or branch (I'm not too clear on the specifics, and honestly it doesn't matter). She's received numerous awards, the greatest of which was being able to get out of surmounting debt that was incurred in the early years of her and my father's marriage.

But the journey was not always sunshine and daisies. During my early childhood, our family lived in a 600 square foot apartment with one bathroom for the four of us to share. My brother was in high school and had to share a bunk bed with his six-year-old brother, and our bedroom didn't have a door. My mom was driving anywhere from forty minutes to four hours for work, depending on which snapshot of the timeline you're looking at, oftentimes having to stay for a week or more in a different city than us.

She has told me that during this time she felt so tired, all the time. How maybe, if she just wrecked her car, injured herself somehow, maybe she'd get a break. Maybe she'd get to rest. But she couldn't. She felt as if there was a monster chasing behind her and that if she wasn't running as hard and fast as she could, it would catch her, and she would lose everything. Maybe even her life.

Later in life, when things slowed a bit (and I cannot emphasize how little), due to some more comforts, the nature of the monster changed. It had now taken the form of younger, fresh-out-of-college students, or notoriously hard-working Indian immigrants, finding work in corporate America and threatening to take her position if she wasn't constantly being the best. Good news was, dad had found a better way to make money and the monster formed by competition didn't seem to run as fast. At least, not at first.

Over the course of their twenty-ish years of marriage, mom and dad had been able to work their way out of what amounts to sheer poverty, most of which I was too young to remember or wasn't around for, and had amassed enough wealth to place us securely in the middle class. Dad owned his own booming business, mom was working hard but thriving, and I was going to school and playing football, while my brother had just started his career in the military. Enter the 2008 housing market crash. Dad lost most of his small business, due to it being based on the new housing market, and our lifestyle fell squarely on my mother's shoulders. The monster was back again.

So where are they now? Mom and dad are in their mid-fifties, in a larger house, with nicer cars, and financially healthier than they have ever been. But they didn't get there on luck. They got there, specifically mom, because she persevered. She faced mounting depression, crippling anxiety, and fear that she could lose everything, most important of which was her family.

Want to know a secret? One that mom would tell you straight to your face if she could? She's not special. There is nothing about her that makes her any different than you, or me, or Joe Blow from down the street. She made it through all of that without a therapist, without a bunch of medication, without dying (God forbid), off of the willpower to persevere.

Here's another secret. You have it too. This willpower has a better word for it. This word literally means "the strength of your character." It is what my mom has, what I have, and what you can have if you win the mental fight against yourself to have it.

It's called *Grit*.

Passion and desire will help you find direction. They'll help you set the course and start the journey, but the only way you'll ever make it to the finish line is if you have grit. The only way you will persevere through the tough times, and adhere to that standard, that natural moral law, the only way you can make sure you don't take a short cut, and cut out the Godliness and the mutual affection, and the love, is if you have grit.

For those of you who take Godliness as a strict adherence to the commands of God because you believe in Him, you are at a major advantage when it comes to perseverance. The reason for that is you always have a coach in your corner to help you. You not only have a guiding light, but you have a greater reason than anyone to chase after your goals and dreams. If you believe, as I do, that God gave everyone a gift and a purpose, then you know that you can persevere through any challenge because any challenge that is greater than you is not greater than God! You can keep walking and keep pressing and keep persevering toward your goal even when the hard times come. Even when it doesn't feel good. Even when it's hard, or seems impossible, because you know in your bones that God has a mission and purpose for you in this life and you will not submit to your fears, your anxieties, or your depression because there is a God that sent you and will see you through!

Like I said at the beginning of this part of the book, I know this because I've lived it. As I write this very part of the book, we sit in quarantine due to COVID-19 and the isolation has prompted the greatest battle against depression that I have ever faced. But I was sent with a purpose. I was sent with a message, and I will not stop because I have been commanded to have faith and follow.

This is my Godliness. This is my perseverance. This is what it looks like to have grit. I'm not special. You can do it too.

SELF-DISCIPLINE

This concept should be easy to grasp, though not easy to do. If you understand perseverance, then you understand self-discipline. What makes self-discipline different, and harder, than perseverance is that perseverance is aimed at the external, whereas self-discipline is internal. Perseverance deals with what is happening to you. Self-discipline deals with what you are doing to yourself.

People often don't realize how much they harm and hinder themselves. You do it with your self-talk, the actions you take, the people you surround yourself with, the habits you allow yourself to develop. It all comes back to self-discipline.

Jocko Willink, one of the great podcasters and leadership coaches of the twenty-first century likes to say that "(self-) discipline is the way to freedom." In other words, if you have no self-discipline, you are not actually free. You're a slave to your own desires. You have to be able to control your desires, analyze objectively whether something is good or bad for you, then make a choice to act. If you act on every desire you have, then you're going to end up in prison, and that's a fact. One of the great divides between humanity and the rest of the animal kingdom is our ability to tame ourselves: our ability to suppress our carnal desires and think logically, regardless of our immediate wants.

Don't be a slave to yourself. He who masters himself can master the world. Learn to persevere against yourself, against your unhealthy desires, so that you may better focus on the task before you. It's not complicated. It's difficult. You can do it though. Your ability to harness your gift depends on it.

KNOWLEDGE

You want to Git Gud? You better have some knowledge. Plain and simple. But you can't get to knowledge without the other steps, so let's review.

We start with love.

Once we know what we love, we surround ourselves with people that we love, and people that love us. Like-minded people. People who will support us and hold us accountable, and for whom we desire to do the same.

Then we find Godliness. We find our objective standard of life, naturally present in the world, and if you choose to believe as I do, handed down from God on high. It's your moral compass, and your coach in your corner.

Then you learn to persevere against the world. When you move to fulfill God's purpose for you, and for those who don't believe in God we can call it destiny, the world will throw everything it can at you from the most sideways places you could imagine. It'll make friends look like foes, foes look like friends, and it'll beat you to the ground with fear, anxiety and depression, as hard as it freaking can. But you won't give in, and you won't give up.

But once you've learned to keep the world from beating you, you have to remember not to beat yourself! You cannot be a slave to your own desires. You must learn to persevere against yourself. This is self-discipline, and if you don't learn it, you will never Git Gud.

But once you learn to master your own desires you have to gain knowledge. You have to learn your craft!

In his book "Outliers" Malcolm Gladwell said it takes 10,000 hours of practice to become a master at something. Last I checked you don't stumble your way to 10,000 hours of anything, save for maybe sleeping and breathing. If you want to master your gift, you need to master it. Gain knowledge in it. Knowledge is power, and your gift will be powerful if you're willing to deny yourself and put in the work to master it.

You have to start somewhere though, so let's lay it out. Where are the places that you can gain knowledge?

1) Find a Coach.

A master. A mentor. Someone to apprentice under. Find them. There will be things you cannot teach yourself because you don't know what you don't know. That's not a typo. You don't know what you don't know. Find someone who knows what you don't know. Then get them to teach you.

As a stipulation to this, you better be willing to pay for the knowledge. Not only should you expect to pay some money, but you should also want to. That person is giving you their time and expertise. If you're worried about the cash in your pocket more than mastering your craft, your priorities are in the wrong place.

2) Read a book.

I swear, the more technology and Netflix and video games take over the world, the less people are reading. People are more than willing to complain that they don't make enough money, wish they knew how to manage their finances better, or wish they knew how to invest their money, yet they won't read a book. Countless studies have been done now, and the evidence is clear: the people who read make more money, are happier, and are more successful in life. Still, everyone wants to make up excuses all the time for why they don't read. "I don't like it," or "I don't have time."

Wrong.

The real reason? Reading is hard and you're lazy.

Who you become over the course of your life is dictated by two things: the people you meet and the things you read.

Stop being lazy. Read a book. Master your craft.

3) Practice.

I won't be that guy and write it three times in a row, but I will say that if you're not willing to practice, you'll never be a master and you'll take your gift to the grave. You'll add to the wealth of the cemetery. You'll need a tombstone when you die, and if this is the reason you're not remembered, I hope you have engraved on that tombstone: "Didn't want to practice."

Freaking practice.

4) Teach someone.

In the same way that you don't know what you don't know, there are some things you can only learn by teaching. Ask any teacher ever and they'll tell you that often times they feel like they're learning more from their students than their students are from them.

Not only does teaching someone help you learn from the person you're teaching, but it solidifies to memory what you already know in ways that you wouldn't expect. You're forced to think of new ways to explain things, which makes them work differently in your own head, too. And it will force you to practice, because otherwise you'll be embarrassed when you make a fool of yourself in front of your student, whether they realize it or not.

Trust me. Been there, done that. Not fun.

Teaching is great, though. And it guarantees that you won't be taking your gift to the grave with you, because there will be someone left on earth to continue your legacy.

Remember: Give unto others, that others may give. Especially knowledge.

GOODNESS

You're done! That's it! You do those things and you Git Gud!

Just kidding. There's one more step. I might call this "Git Gud", but the equation isn't about goodness, it's about your gift. It's about your craft. It's about your goals and dreams and aspirations. For us to really master these things, we have to also master goodness.

Now, goodness is broken into two parts. First, there is the moral side of goodness, then there's the technical side of goodness.

We've been talking a lot about morality so let's take a break from that and tackle the technical side of things first.

Technical goodness, the actual act of "getting good", occurs when you combine your passion (your love) with the knowledge you've gained through your journey, and your technical proficiency.

See, when it comes to the realm of gifts, if you don't love something, then you're probably not going to stick with it very long. That being said, you could love something and have zero knowledge about the subject, and so every time you attempt to act on that love, the outcome is mediocre. It's not what it could be if you were to apply a knowledge of the craft to your action.

In the same way, you could love something, and spend your whole life learning about it and gaining knowledge, and never put it to action. You could be too afraid, you could be buying into the world's lie that you have to be lucky to do something you love, you could be buying into other lies, like "you're not good enough," "you're not smart enough," "no one will follow you," or my personal favorite, "you suck."

Don't fall for this bull. You're not special, but neither is most of the world, and those that are aren't going to berate you for using your gift. They'll be encouraging you to keep going and keep doing because that's what the truly special people do.

Three things.

Love.

Knowledge.

Action.

Follow the formula, put these together, and you'll make it. You'll begin to actually use your gifts.

But who are you using them for? Is it yourself? Is the goal self-satisfaction? Or are you trying to make the world a better place? Are you trying to influence others and show them that they can do the same?

I'm going to use two polar extremes here to illustrate a point of goodness, and I need you to buy in.

In all of history, I can think of no better examples than Mahatma Gandhi and Adolf Hitler as men who used their gift for influencing people.

Like I said. Polar ends of the spectrum.

Both men were gifted in their ability to articulate their dreams and thoughts. Both men amassed a massive following, and both men forever changed the landscape of our world with their gifts.

One used his gift to bring about the liberation of an oppressed people from an imperialist British society.

One used his gift to coerce his followers into murdering an estimated 14.8 million people during the Holocaust.

How do you wish to use your gifts? How do you want your ideas to shape the future? Do you want to just "Git Gud"? Or do you actually want to *be good*?

The first line of our formula says to "add to your faith goodness." The Rock isn't just talking about excellence in action; he's talking about excellence in morals. If you're not morally grounded, the efforts and impacts of your gift mean nothing.

You'll be forgotten like one that took their gift to the grave, or you'll be used in another book like this one as an example of what *not* to do, just like I used Hitler.

Don't be like Hitler.

Be like Gandhi.

Be *good*.

Give unto others.

ROCK SOLID

The Rock was a heck of a guy. He was an amazing scholar and believed so much in his ideals that he was martyred for them. And it wasn't a clean death. No beheading, guillotine, or hanging. He wasn't shot, because guns weren't invented yet. He wasn't assassinated or poisoned. The Rock didn't even get to die by fire, where it would be excruciating till his nerves burned away. No, his death was worse.

He was publicly humiliated in the middle of Rome during the reign of the Roman Emperor Nero by being crucified *upside down*. We sleep on the atrocity of crucifixion today. Most people know it was bad, but they underestimate how bad until the process is described to them. It starts with days of torture. The most common during The Rock's time was a public flogging. The whips used would be barbed with metal and thorns so they would rip the skip with each lash. The flogging was so intense and brutal that the victim's spine and internal organs would be visible by someone standing feet away. After the flogging, the victims would be forced to carry the wooden cross that they would die upon through the streets till they reached the place that the crucifixion would occur. Here, the victim would be forced to lay on the cross as iron nails were driven with wooden mallets into their ankle joints and the wrist, just behind the joint where all the tendons and veins are. This severs the victim's tendons in the wrist and ankle and causes excruciating pain, but not as much as what comes next. After the victim has been nailed to the cross, it is hoisted vertically and planted in the ground like a tree. The victim's weight pulls as the puncture wounds of the nails and causes their shoulders to dislocate from the weight and awkward position. The lungs are pressed upon and breathing becomes impossible unless the victim uses their legs to push on the nail holding their feet to the cross long enough to take a breath. Often, this would cause the shoulders to relocate briefly, but when the weak and bleeding person would sag back down, the shoulders would dislocate again, causing more pain. Eventually, the victim would die by suffocation, either because they were too weak to try or because they survived too long, and the legionaries would shatter their shin bones so they could no longer bear weight.

Petros, our Rock, knew this is what awaited him. It is speculated that he even requested the inverted version because he did not want to die in the same way as Jesus of Nazareth.

I add this piece in here because the formula we just discussed was written in one of the letters The Rock wrote that led to his death. By extension, this formula, this teaching, is one of the things he died for.

Not only that, but if you follow this formula, you will find that it's not just good in theory. It's as solid in practice as the faith of the man who died for it.

So, who was he?

The Rock, as we discussed earlier, claimed the Greek name of Petros, a name that in English translates to "Peter".

You might have guessed this by now, but here it is. The author of the letters who provides the formula for getting good at anything in your life was Peter. The same Peter that Jesus looked at and said, "Upon this rock I shall build my church."

You have the formula now. You know how to Git Gud. Now I have two more words of encouragement for you.

Don't suck.

DON'T SUCK

"**D**on't Suck" was actually the first motivational speech I ever wrote. I was writing it before I ever had the idea to found Forerunner Productions, before the podcast was even a thought, and before I had made up my mind that I was going to become a career public speaker. All I had was a calling on my life, a gift of being so loud people couldn't help but hear me, and a message on my heart that could never have come from just me, which needed to be shared with the world. Matter of fact, I was just coming out of one of the low points in my life, where I was confronted again with the recurring feeling of being a complete and utter failure. Let me break it down for you.

This part of the story starts after the failure of my small business. I was a ballroom dance instructor and was the majority owner in a small studio that was a part of a franchise that spanned from Boca Raton, Florida, to Carrie, North Carolina. Due to a long series of events, the likes of which I won't confuse you with because it's more complicated than HBO's "Game of Thrones" (you know, before it went to crap in season eight), I found myself declaring bankruptcy and walking away from what I thought would be my life-long career.

After the business went under, I thought I would go into real estate, but due to another series of unforeseen complications, I felt God calling me to serve my country. I knew from the time I was six, after watching my brother play games like Ghost Recon and SOCOM: US Navy SEALs, that if I were to ever join the armed services I would do so as a member of the Special Operations community. Lucky for me, I got a head start, because my brother was already a part of that community. He had been doing the job I wanted to do for thirteen years.

Fast forward through an amazing time living with him and his wife and getting to love all over my gorgeous nieces, and through basic training and an eight week hell show we called Battlefield Airmen Preparatory Course, as well as the Tactical Air Control Party Preparatory Course, and I found myself in the hardest training I had ever experienced.

And I was thriving. I loved it. I was obsessed with the suck, I loved the teamwork and camaraderie with my team, and I had the pleasure of being on team with some of the best leaders I think I will ever find.

Then I got kicked out. I made a dumb choice. We were told not to speak while out on a training exercise and I broke that rule by non-verbally communicating by a whistle and wave to a Sergeant that was nearby. My reasons don't matter, the circumstances don't either. Bottom line is I broke the rules of engagement. Do that down range and you get yourself, or worse, your team, killed. I was gone, removed from the program.

Once again, I was left feeling as though I had failed.

It was in the aftermath of picking myself up by my bootstraps and refusing to lie down, refusing to be mediocre, refusing to let my gift be added to the wealth of the cemetery, that I remembered something my brother had told me over and over and over again.

Don't Suck.

It's something we still say to each other to this day, but it means something different to me now. I hope, by the end of this section, it'll mean something different to you too.

WHAT DOES THAT MEAN?

When he started telling me "Don't suck", I'm ninety percent certain that my brother just thought it sounded cool. The ten percent of doubt comes from the fact that my brother is five times more intelligent than I am, so there's a slight possibility that he spent more than ten seconds thinking about the actual semantics and not just the syntax. Regardless of whether he did or not, if I were to ever ask him, "Hey Rich, what does 'don't suck' mean?" I am positive he would look at me with his "are you stupid" face and say, "It means don't suck. Beat it, nerd."

If you can't tell, he's a delicate man with all the articulate grace of a wildebeest in a priceless art museum.

Needless to say, I didn't ask my brother. But I was curious; what does it mean? Or at least, what would a common websearch tell me it means? See, I was looking for a starting place to begin my speech and breaking down the specifics of the language seemed important to me at the time.

Off to trusty Google.com I went, and here's what I got.

To suck;
be very bad, disagreeable, or disgusting.

Okay, this didn't really help. I tried to make it fit eight ways from Sunday, and eventually gave up.

The reality is, as many of you will realize in your lives, that you tend to already have the answers you're looking for. When it comes to the meaning of words you've used your whole life, or the answer to a moral quandary, or what choice to make in regard to an action that would have any amount of consequence, you already have the answer. We go looking for an answer in other places for several reasons.

One of them is that we don't like the answer we've given ourselves. It's kind of like visiting a doctor and requesting a second opinion on the likelihood that cancer will kill you; sometimes, we can't come to terms with the truth, especially if it comes from within us.

A second reason we look for other answers is because we lack the self-confidence necessary to trust our own judgment. This skepticism can be healthy if you have a more reliable source at the ready with which to check yourself, but I hate to tell you the Internet doesn't qualify.

There are more, but the last reason I'll list here is we have the humility to admit that we don't know what we're talking about, so we ignore our knee-jerk reactions and inclinations till we have better perspective.

It's so easy to get these mixed up, though. Even as a self-proclaimed 'writer', I often find myself struggling with both syntax and semantics. So, when it came time to voice thoughts about this life principle that my brother shared, I thought I needed to get a better perspective. I thought I needed more knowledge before I presented myself as an expert on the subject. What did my search reward me with?

Don't be very bad.

Don't be disagreeable.

Don't be disgusting.

Go ahead. Try and apply those to your life in a meaningful way. Ten bucks says you can't. We're all going to be 'very bad' at something. So long as it's not morally, I think you'll be okay. We're all going to be disagreeable with someone or something at some point, because if you're agreeable all the time it means you don't stand for anything, and as I'll talk about later, that's the exact opposite of what 'Don't suck' actually means. And we should all hope to not be disgusting. Hygiene is important, but there's more to 'Don't suck' than 'take a freaking shower and brush your teeth'.

As it turns out, when I started my search, I wasn't falling under the knowledge reason, I was actually falling under the first reason. I wanted a second opinion because I feared what it would mean after I taught the lesson. I would be accountable to my own teaching, and what I'm about tell you to do is hard. If the rest of this book wasn't hard, then this will be. It's something I've struggled with my whole life, something I'm still working on to this day. At times, I find myself being a hypocrite to my own lesson and I have to correct myself, or more often than not, rely on my closest friends and community to correct me.

What does it mean?

It means 'don't abandon your standard.'

STANDARDS

Let's rewind the clock again. I just got told by the Cadre out at our field training exercise to pack up my crap and get back to base camp. I was in a truck that evening, heading back to our dorms to wait while the Cadre and the Commander of the schoolhouse decided what to do with me, but I think in my heart I knew it was over. I've never been the person that life gives second chances to. It's always been one and done for me. This was no different. Whatever hope I had was false hope, and it showed itself with what I did when I got back to my room.

I hadn't showered in four days so my first priority was to get the water hot so I could deprogram as the water rinsed the grime from my body. Most people would have been focused on getting a good meal after eating nothing but MREs for four days. Some might have thought about doing laundry to get the smell out of their uniform. All I could think about was, "What is Richie going to say?" I had let down my brother, my hero. Sure, some people in his career field didn't like him, but from what I gathered from the majority, he had built a helluva reputation as being a solid dude, a go-getter, a badass, for lack of a better term. It was a reputation I had paid for time and time again, in good ways, funny ways. One that I had done a decent job of upholding during my time in training.

And it was a reputation I felt I had soiled the moment I decided to break the Rules of Engagement.

After my shower, the whole time of which I spent thinking about what I would say to him, I sat on my bed and wrote a long, apologetic text message. I didn't call him. I wouldn't have known what to say the moment I heard his voice. I don't think I could have handled the conversation anyway. Text message it was. The coward's way out.

My brother isn't one for sob stories. I was also sure that he already knew about what had happened, due to his connections in the schoolhouse, so explaining everything to him would be overkill. I tried to keep it short. Still ended up longer than I would have liked, and it probably annoyed him more than anything to read it, but he did. And his reply is what led to this whole thing. This lesson. My company. The podcast. My degree path. My career path. All of it.

This is what it said:

Stop living based on what I think. Make your own decisions and live up to your own standard, not mine. Don't worry about disappointing me. You do you.

Whose standard are you living by?

Some of the greatest people to have ever lived, the ones who are truly special, had to live by their own standard, too. We wouldn't know their names if they hadn't.

Shakespeare invented words which had never existed before and wrote stories that captivated audiences in ways the likes of which had never been seen before, even dating back to Greek theater. He faced scrutiny, and worst of all, is believed to have been plagued with crippling depression. He still decided to live by a standard that immortalized his name for the good things he created in this world.

Stephen Hawking went to college at eleven years old. He was awarded his doctorate when he was twenty-one and had ideas and proved things mathematically that would have made Einstein's head spin. The same year he was awarded his doctorate, Dr. Hawking was also diagnosed with ALS (Lou Gehrig's disease). Dr. Hawking spent most of his adult life confined to a wheelchair, speaking through a robot. As his nerves died, his limbs would tingle and burn. Eventually, he lost his ability to eat solid food, and one day, the disease would make its way to his lungs, and he would no longer be able to breathe. To most people, this life isn't one worth living, yet Dr. Hawking set a standard for his life that he lived up to unto his dying breath.

Let's look at someone who isn't special. Someone like you and me.

Denzel Washington, the one who's won 39 different awards in his acting career, once auditioned for a play on Broadway early in his career. He was rejected. Didn't get the role. He could have quit. Could have been dejected and downtrodden and taken the back seat while someone else would go on to win all those awards in future. But he didn't. He had a higher standard, one that didn't match societies. One that wouldn't accept anything other than greatness. 30 years later he was in a play on Broadway called 'Fences'. It won all sorts of awards and holds a dear place in Mr. Washington's heart. That play was held in the Court Theater. The same theater he had failed at thirty years prior.

Whose standard are you playing by?

I want to take this a step further with you.

The only standard that should matter is the standard you set for yourself.

Be warned: your standard will determine your outcome. A low standard has a low ceiling.

I word it like that specifically because there are two parts to setting a standard.

First, understanding that our joy and contentment in this

world is decided by not being bogged down by trivialities that fall outside our standard is paramount. If we don't master this, then we're not actually playing by our own standard. We must learn to let go.

Second, the quality of our standard matters. Sure, we could keep rolling with the standard that society wants us to believe in: that we have to get lucky to be wealthy or happy or have a good life. That greatness can't be achieved through hard work. That life is supposed to be easy, and when it's not, it's someone else's fault. Or, we could take ownership of our standard. Decide for yourself what is important and stick to it.

My standard has several parts. The first is I choose to follow the rules and laws of the Bible, the standard exhibited by the life of Jesus the Christ. The second is that I refuse to quit. I am a man of ambition, and so long as there is something left for me to achieve, a new goal to strive for, I will not back down, lie down, or give up. I will fail till I die if I so must, but I will breathe my last breath before I give up. Next, I will protect those I love. My family, my friends, and those who choose to follow me. Lastly, the mission statement of my life that guides my ambition. Give unto others, that others may give.

Do you have a standard? What things are most important to you that you refuse to back down on? How does it let you use your gift and influence the world?

You may not have the answers yet, but you will if you think about it long and hard.

I also encourage you to write a mission statement. Writing my own was some of the best advice I was ever given by a close friend, and since doing so it has helped tremendously in maintaining my standard. I'm sure it will help you too.

UNITY

Not sure how many times I've said it now, but I'm going to keep saying it until it sinks in. You need other people. You need a community of support around you. Like the header of this segment alludes to, I want to focus on the last five letters of community. The "Unity" part of it.

Unity has two main derivatives that are imperative to your success in using your gifts.

The first is 'Unify'. When you think of this, I want you to think internal: you need to unify the broken pieces within yourself.

Every person gets hurt in life. Every person experiences pain. Some of us are subjected to more of it than others, but we can all relate on the level of having contacted some element of pain in our life. This pain causes us to fragment internally. It breaks us, tears at us, and sometimes we let our internal self lie in pieces. If we are to make the most of our gifts, we cannot allow ourselves to remain fragmented. We must learn to pick up the broken pieces of ourselves and heal.

This healing takes many forms. A lot of it has to do with forgiveness. Some of it will have to be reconciliation. You might have to develop new habits to get over some of it or help someone with their pain to help heal part of your own. Whatever it takes, you have to be willing to open yourself to the healing.

And though it is a topic for another book, I will mention here that there are some wounds that can only be healed by a higher power.

I'm not naive enough to tell you that you'll be the same as you were before the pain. You won't. The pieces of the puzzle don't fit back together the same way they fell apart; that's not how the human soul works. But if you're willing to heal and find a new way to put the pieces together, you'll come back stronger than ever before. That's called growth. You can't grow without pain. It's a hard fact. But those who grow the most learn to embrace the pain and learn how to heal faster and stronger with each encounter that makes its attempt at their soul.

You'll never master this, though. Each new encounter with pain, each new thing that breaks you will feel brand new. That's okay. You're stronger than you think, better than you give yourself credit for. And though you'll never master this, you'll have no chance at success in the second part of Unity if you don't at least begin the journey of mending.

You don't have to be perfect. I don't care if you ever finish the journey of healing. None of that matters unless you start the journey first. I just need you to start.

The second part of Unity is 'Union'. When you think 'Union', I want you to think external. Companionship. Create a union around you. You'll only ever be so strong on your own. Together with other people who can fill your blind spots and make up for your weaknesses, there's no limit to what you can achieve.

But if you haven't begun to heal from your hurt, it will be increasingly difficult for you to form this union. People can sense when those around us are broken. Part of this sixth sense makes us want to help that person. Some people even have this innate ability to seek out broken spirits. It's their gift. It might be yours. The only downside to this ability to sense brokenness is that though we want to help, it makes it difficult for us to trust those people. Why this is, I can only speculate. My best guess is that until someone accepts their brokenness, they aren't being honest with themselves. And if they can't be honest with themselves, how can we trust them to be honest with us? The answer is that we can't, not fully, because it doesn't seem genuine. But once we start that journey and accept our broken nature, it is easier to carry ourselves upright. It's easier to be genuine to other people. It's easier for us to trust and to be trusted. Honesty starts in the heart. When you're honest with yourself, it bleeds out of you into your interactions with others.

This genuine nature is necessary to build a union. Why? Because part of building a union, of having companions, of having a community, is to have people who genuinely care about you enough to call you out on your crap when we live in a society that tells you to leave people alone. That they aren't your problem. A "you do you" society. A selfish society.

Screw that. Find people who will call you on your crap. Find people who care about your well-being enough to hurt your feelings in order to better you. Find people who will grab you by the collar of your shirt and hold on to you, and even drag you behind them if they need to, when you start to stray from the right path. When you start to get let go of your standard.

It'll only happen if you've learned how to heal. It'll only happen if you find the people who actually care. Don't be passive about this. Be wary, but actively seek these people out. If more people would give a crap like this, there would be a lot fewer problems in the world.

Make up your mind that you give a crap.

Make up your mind to have Unity in your life.

CHAMPIONS & CHALLENGES

When you imagine a champion, what do you see?

For me, it's your typical fantasy image: some cross between Roman gladiator, medieval knight, battered and bloody Viking, smashed together with weapons and armor that themselves are a ridiculous mix of Final Fantasy, Dark Souls, and

Dungeons and Dragons. Pretty dorky, right? For you, it might be something as simple as a historical figure. Take the group the Knights Templar. They were a band of outcast warriors who loved God and were founded to protect the travelers on the road from brigands. If that doesn't suit your fancy, you could always look to a prominent fictional character who can sometimes be more real to us than anything in history. Like Rocky, standing in the ring, arms held high, screaming Adrian's name after the fight of his life. Regardless of what you choose to imagine, all champions have something in common: they all stand for something. Whether they want to or not, because of their actions and because of their beliefs, the mere image of them comes to represent something.

The moment you make the choice to change your outlook on life and unify those around you, and unify the desires within you, you forfeit your ability to sit in the stands and be a bystander. Those around you will begin to notice the change, maybe even before you notice it yourself. This is because the unification turns you into a force for your beliefs. A champion for your standards.

To some, this seems scary. Don't worry. People aren't going to start erecting statues of you simply because you carry yourself differently and have unlocked the potential to be supremely effective at using your gift. As a matter of fact, you can actually expect the opposite to happen. More often than not, you'll be faced with opposition instead of welcome. This is because people who stand for something are threatening to those who stand for nothing. The aura given off by someone who lives free of the crushing weight of mediocre standards put forth by the world is daunting and intimidating to most people. Guess what?

That's okay.

Here's how you handle that. Make part of your standard one of love and tolerance. Even if you are setting out to right evils and bring justice to the world and all that gooey chivalrous stuff, make sure you leave room for grace and tolerance.

Just because you've unlocked this potential to not suck like the majority of society doesn't mean you have a free pass to look down on people. Let's look back at our examples from before.

The weird fantasy guy I imagined didn't get to where he was by being a jerk. He wasn't born into a position of power. He wasn't given talent with a blade by some deity, making him an arena champion. He worked for it. Cared for people. Protected people. In his story, he started in a wheelchair, unable to get to the bathroom by himself because of an accident.

Let's get out of my fantasy world and go to history. The Templars were outcasts. Lords who had no claim to land, criminals who were given a choice of death or servitude to the order, the list goes on. Once they earned their tunic, with a crimson cross, they set out to do what? Protect peasants and other travelers on the roads between the towns and cities. Their place in society was like a Knight without a fiefdom, yet they dedicated their lives to protecting those who could not protect themselves and serving a cause that was great than themselves. Even when misguided, the servitude to the Order was by-and-large selfless.

What about Rocky? Did Rocky start spitting on the plebeians when he won his fight against Apollo Creed? No! He was part of the Philly working class. He settled in his small town. Kept the woman he loved from the pet store as his wife. He didn't go off with his head in the clouds, looking down on everyone that helped him get there, but because of what he stood for, (hard work, dedication, perseverance) the people around him looked at Rocky differently.

Sadly, to say, merely standing for something isn't enough. Making the choice, changing your view, and living by your own standards with a unified community and unity inside yourself will make you a symbol, sure. But you're more than a symbol. Next, we talk about how you're going to embody that next level.

KINESTHETIC

Kinesthetic - "Relating to a person's awareness of the position and movement of the parts of the body by means of sensory organs (proprioceptors) in the muscles and joints." That's the literal dictionary definition of Kinesthetic if you couldn't guess, and the bottom line is that it all relates to movement.

It's not enough that you can stand for something. People stand for things all the time. They stand in line at the store, waiting to check out their groceries. They stand in the kitchen while they wait for their leftovers to get done in the microwave. The really cool ones, like my fantasy guy, get to stand in the middle of an arena with giant banner that lets everyone know who he is and what he stands for. Less cool things like billboards are built to stand for long periods of time. Billboards especially can not only stand for something, but they can say some stuff too, based on who wants to advertise on that segment of road.

My point is that it's not enough to merely stand. You don't just get to be a champion, a symbol, and not do anything with it. Do that, and you've managed to get through three-fourths of this entire thing and still suck at the end of it. No, if you don't want to suck, if you really want to live by your own standard and make the most of your gift, you've got to be kinesthetic. You have to move. You have to act. You have to do something.

The Bible says, "Faith without works is dead." This doesn't mean you don't get into heaven without doing good deeds. Anyone that tells you that doesn't actually read the bible. What it does mean, however, is that if you genuinely believe something, then you will want to act on it. It's a direct correlation to what scholars call Orthodoxy (what you believe) and Orthopraxy (what you do). If you honestly believe in the standard that you have chosen for yourself, you'll act on it.

Being kinesthetic in your championing of those ideals will be easy. If you haven't fully bought into that standard by which you want to live, then it'll be hard justifying the actions that must be taken when it's hard.

Do you believe you can break the cycle of alcoholism that has plagued your family? Then giving up drinking for good will happen, even when it isn't easy.

Do you really believe you can be the first person in your family to graduate college? Then waking up and getting to class will happen, even when it isn't easy.

Do you believe that you can be the good father you never had? Then you'll make it to your son's football game, even if it costs you that promotion.

Do you want to be a better wife to your husband than your mother was as you watch her cheat on your dad time and time again? Then you'll say no to the advances of the dashing man who sweet talks you when things feel like they are falling apart with your husband.

These are just a few examples of hard choices life (and Lucifer) can throw at us when we're vulnerable and feel like we need to give up. Don't fall for it. You're better than that, and there are people you can't see in your life who see you in a way that you could never imagine, people who may be on the cusp of becoming a champion themselves. They look to you for strength now because you've become their champion. You don't have to do anything crazy to succeed in this. Just don't give in. Don't back down when things get tough. Take action and be kinesthetic toward your goals and standards. As Jocko Willink says, "Discipline is freedom." Be disciplined. Be free. Live your standard.

FULL CIRCLE

That's it. Don't Suck. Standards, Unity, Champion and Kinesthetic. Sounds kind of corny, but I'm sure you'll remember it. Especially after this last bit.

Remember our champion? The fantasy one? And the Templars, remember them to? As a matter of fact, let's look at every champion in the medieval period. When champions went to war, they always took something with them. Often they would have someone else carry it for them. This item let the enemy know where they were on the field, and it was a challenge to anyone that opposed them, saying, "Here I am! Best me if you can!" This item carried their identity, their history, and their lineage with it. It inspired those around them and struck fear in those that could not carry the same.

Some call it a flag.

Others call it a banner.

I call it a Standard.

"But Chad, what happens if I still suck? I got my standard, I'm unified, I'm championing my ideals and I'm acting on what I believe in, but I still failed. I still suck. Should I give up?"

You're going to hate me. I hate to say it, but even the best of us still have bad days. Once you're living by your own standard, the only person left to really disappoint is yourself. Sadly, it's going to happen. The answer to how you deal with that failure is really simple to say and extremely hard for most of us to accomplish, especially since society teaches us now that if something is hard, just take an easier road. That ain't the answer.

The answer is this:

Crush the coward inside of you that says, "Give up."

Take a breath. It's okay to breathe sometimes.
Pick yourself up.
Try again, and suck less.

CRUSH THE COWARD

I mentioned at the end of the last chapter a phrase that I don't want you to miss out on. *Crush the Coward.* This is something that I learned in high school and it's gotten me through the toughest, and scariest times of my life. Once I break it down, maybe it'll help you the same way, too.

I started hearing this phrase from a former coach of mine. For the sake of his privacy, I'll just call him Coach from here on out.

I was probably a Sophomore the first time I heard Coach say the phrase, and it quickly became a staple that our team heard over and over again throughout the years. It sounded like something my older brother would say, which is probably why I listened to it. The context of the phrase "crush the coward" came in regard to how we worked out.

Our coach was our weightlifting coach, and also headed up the offensive line, and was the junior varsity head coach. In all honesty, he scared the piss out of me. Still does to an extent. He had ice-blue eyes that would pierce your soul when he got mad, which was more often than not, though he did have a good sense of humor as well. He was one of those fifty-fifty guys. There was rarely an in-between: he was either pissed to high hell, and we were going to pay for it, or he was in a great mood, and we would pay for that too. Either way, every other day, during third block, we knew we were going to have our asses handed to us in the weight room or doing sprints in the sand pit or bus lot right outside. Believe it or not, the high school football workouts I went to were harder than ninety percent of what I did in college, and the only thing that made the military more intense was the attitude of our cadre, because our literal lives hung in the balance down range, not just a football game on Friday night. Coach did his best to, whether intentionally or not, get the intensity as close to that life or death place as he could, though. Lots of potentially good athletes never played for him because of it. To him, they were cowards.

Pretty insensitive, right? That's just who Coach was though. Not a lot of feeling, not a lot of emotion (besides anger and a few laughs), and whole lot of "crush the coward and do it." Needless to say, I don't exactly want to go down that road with you. I may be abrasive, but I do have a heart. Promise.

Though Coach was a bit insensitive, I think he was really on to something with the whole "crush the coward" thing, and the more I've thought about it, the more merit I've discovered it has, especially in the context of using our gifts.

The concept goes like this. Inside everyone is the bravery to step out and do something great. There is a gift that needs to be used and a want to use it. Sadly, along with that brave persona and all that potential, there is also a coward within us as well. You know what I'm talking about by that much, I'm sure, but I'll take it a step farther for you. Every time you hear the voice in your head that says, "That's too hard," "I can't," "There's no way," you're hearing the coward within you speak. The coward rarely says, "I'm afraid." Matter of fact, it avoids that language as much as possible, because the recognition of the truth is the first step to beating this thing. Rather, it will feed you lies formed by fear, anxiety, and depression, and it'll do its damnedest to keep you in that box.

The worst part is, you listen. Not because you want to be afraid, or because you really believe that you can't do something, but because within the fear and the grasp of the coward is the illusion of safety. This safety is the safety of a prison, though.

Sure, there are thick walls, and security guards, but your freedom is restricted and your potential stifled. It's the prison of your own mind, the manifestation of your fear, anxiety, and depression, and though you think that this prison is protecting you from the failure and hurt that would breed more fear and anxiety and depression, what this coward is doing is feeding you those things to keep you locked away.

In this chapter, I want talk about that fear, anxiety, and depression. I want to talk about what they feel like, what can cause those feelings, and some basic methods to keep the coward from getting out of control.

Fair warning: some of this will be tough love. I am also not a psychologist or a counselor. If what I say helps you, amazing. If not, and you feel like you are having thoughts of suicide, or like you truly are in a prison of your own mind, more so than what I have described and will illustrate further in, please seek professional medical assistance. The strongest, bravest thing we can ever do in our life is be humble enough to ask for help.

ANXIETY

There's a picture I use when I present "Don't Suck" as a motivational speech that is the best depiction of anxiety I have ever seen. The picture is black and white. It shows a woman screaming, but it's not a clear picture. The picture is blurred, as if catching a motion-capture video in a single shot. Imagine watching the woman scream, thrashing about in fifty different directions, then watching it again in high speed. Now take the high-speed version (like you've doubtlessly seen in a music video somewhere in your life) and put that in a picture. Blurred lines. Chaos. Pain and screaming through frustration and uncertainty. It's profound and it highlights what anxiety does to us, but where does anxiety come from?

I'm saving fear for last, but it's really impossible to talk about anxiety without mentioning fear. That's because anxiety is born of fear. Crazier still, there is not a single thing in our adult lives that we fear that was not first developed at some time in our adolescence. Surprisingly enough, we can break down the stages in which we develop these fears in chunks of our childhood. Several people with doctorate degrees did the research for this (namely K. Beesdo-Baum and S. Knappe in their piece Developmental Epidemiology of Anxiety Disorders); all I did was simplify it into something we regular folk or a regular, non-doctorate of psychology brain can understand. I break up the research into four groups in which we develop anxieties over things that stick with us to varying degrees.

I'll lay out the stages first, and then we can talk about how to crush the coward by tackling them one section at a time.

From ages zero to three, we develop anxieties that I call "The Safe Space" anxieties. These are separation anxieties from our parents and anxieties born of shyness towards strangers. In essence, the things that get us out of our perceived safe space, namely, our parents.

From ages four to six, we enter the realm I call "Crap We Don't Understand" or "Crap We Don't Understand Yet", depending on the item we're talking about. These fears and anxieties are born of a lack of understanding in regard to death, both for ourselves and others, because we are finally old enough to realize the repercussions that death has on people and we are scared of the unknown beyond it should we die ourselves; and in regard to natural things such as thunder, lightning, fire, water, darkness, nightmares, animals, and imaginary creatures.

From ages seven to twelve, we encounter what I call "Fear of the Uncontrollable", as well as a separate issue that most people have experienced in their life, performance anxiety. The reason I talk about the uncontrollable first is because this is the point in life where we realize there are things that we cannot control, even if we learn about them: germs, falling ill, natural disasters, traumatic events, and even harm to self or others. When we talk about actions to crush these, I'll tackle performance anxiety and the uncontrollable separately.

Lastly, we have ages twelve-plus. This section is all about the fear and anxiety that comes with "Attacks on our Pride". The two biggest factors that play into this are peer rejection and negative evaluation. We begin to truly care about what the people around us think about what we do. We begin to establish a self-identity and take pride in that identity. God forbid this identity get critiqued, or someone (whose opinion we value) doesn't agree or support us; we'll take it personally because it hurts our pride.

Naturally, each person is different and some of these may begin to develop earlier in one person than another. Nevertheless, this is the progression we all go through, and as we break down the reasoning behind it so that we may attack the coward where he wants to hit us most, you'll see that the build makes sense.

🏆

THE SAFE SPACE

The Safe Space anxieties are largely dependent on two factors: individual personality and parental influence. Nature versus Nurture. Personally, I find nurture to be more influential in this particular case, because even introverted people can be taught to be sociable if their parents put them in the proper situations. Sadly, there are far too many parents who are overly protective of their children (think Eddie Kaspbrak's mother from Steven King's "IT") or, and I find this to be more common, a failure by parents to be deliberate in exposing their child to a quality amount of separation and interaction with strangers (or better yet, people who might not be strangers but you as a child don't know that, so you see them as a stranger. Same lessons, safer environment.)

But let's assume for a minute that you're already grown, or mostly grown, and you're reading this book thinking, "We'll I'm screwed because my parents didn't do a good job raising me in this particular area," or "I'm screwed because I'm just not made for being away from my parents/family," or (and probably most commonly) "I'm screwed because I suck at interacting with strangers, and just thinking about doing so gives me anxiety." (See what I did there? *wink*)

Well, you're not screwed. You're a little behind the eight-ball, but it's possible to get out with relative ease. How so? Do what your parents didn't do with you. Expose yourself to the separation and to strangers more. Seems like a "duh-huh" plan but trust me it works. But also, don't misunderstand me and think I want you to just jump off the deep end and move out of your parents' house tomorrow. Also don't think that I want you to go to the middle of the inner city and start striking up conversations with any joe-shmo on the sidewalk. No-no, we need baby steps. If separation is your issue, go for a long vacation or hiking trip with friends who feel like family. If it's strangers that weird you out, take a friend with you to a concert or church or a local beach and try striking up a conversation with someone. You don't have to force it, but if you see someone wearing something that you also like, it's not strange to say, "Hey, I like your shirt. Where did you get it?" It's the simple things. It'll be weird, or even hard at first, but you'll only overcome it with exposure.

CRAP WE DON'T UNDERSTAND (YET)

Think about the first time you found out that something was hot as a kid. I mean really found out. Especially if it involved an open flame. Wasn't too fun, was it? What about your experience with water? Were you the type that jumped right in the pool as a kid, or did you take 5 minutes to ease your way in from your ankles to your knees to your waist to your chest like I did? I'm a firm believer that the reason children are scared of things like fire, or water, or thunder and lightning, is because they don't understand them yet. Once we learn why a fire is hot and that we can manipulate and control it, fire inspires far less fear. We still don't want to get burned, but we're not afraid to cook or build a fire while camping because we understand how fire behaves. It becomes predictable. Water is the same way. Pools and lakes are scary at first because we don't know how to manipulate them, and our bodies, to float. We like oxygen, and when we learn the small fact that we can choke on water we're drinking, or suffocate under it in a pool, water becomes a very fear-inspiring thing. But once we learn to swim, and that we can manipulate water to allow us to cook and clean and have fun, it no longer inspires us to fear. Even thunderstorms, complete with crashing bolts of fire that we call lightning, become less scary with education. Once you learn that it's not magic, and that the loud sound has an origin, the lightning loses much of what makes it scary. Sure, the loud crack will startle us, and the knowledge of what lightning can do might inspire a bit of fear, but the knowledge of the statistics that you're more likely to get bitten by a shark than to get struck by lightning makes that aspect less daunting.

The moral, if you haven't figured it out, is education. We overcome these anxieties by educating ourselves on the truths about them. This even goes for the darkness.

I'm a firm believer that when someone says they're scared of the dark, it's not the actual darkness that they fear, but what might be lurking in the darkness. You can prove this by putting someone in a dark corner but have them able to see a room filled with light. The person typically won't mind being in the dark because they can still see all the things happening outside of the dark space they're occupying. In the same vein, you take someone who's scared of the dark and blindfold them in a perfectly lit room and they're likely to lose their mind. Why? It's the perception of the darkness and what our imaginations do with the unknown.

The best horror films I've ever watched didn't show the monster outright until the very end of the movie. Why? Because all great horror artists know that a person's imagination will freak them out a thousand times worse than anything you could show on that screen. This is also why horror is so effective in novel format. The description only takes a person so far, but their imagination takes them over the top. Nightmares work off this same premise: darkness feeds the imagination, the imagination feeds the fear, the fear lingers in our minds and nightmares are born of the things our imagination conjures up.

The secret is still education. By educating ourselves about what is in the darkness, we can keep from feeding our imaginations fuel for the fear and anxiety. By understanding that our fears and anxieties are fueled by our imaginations, we can more easily recognize when our imaginations are getting out of hand. Once we are able to make this objective assessment of ourselves, we then have to train ourselves to detach from the emotions and the ideas that are feeding our imagination so that we can get these things back under control. Great methods for detachment are focused breathing, active prayer and meditation, and (my personal favorite) distraction. Never underestimate the power of an awesome distraction. Video games, good novels, cooking in the kitchen, blasting your favorite music way too loud, anything goes. Just get our mind off the anxiety and on to something else.

Death is a little different, though. The answer is still the same with how we deal with this fear—through education—but your education has to come from a different source than science or a textbook. For all of our technological advancements, our knowledge of death and the afterlife is extremely limited. No living man has ever seen the other side of death and lived to tell the tale. No living man save one.

Out of all the science, all the religions, all the theories and rituals and ideas that people have developed over centuries, only one man has ever been known to have been killed, buried, and come back to tell the world of his experience on the other side. That man was Jesus of Nazareth. There is historical evidence, uncovered by geologists, that proves not only Jesus' existence and his crucifixion, but also his resurrection. Secular sources report that Jesus did in fact appear to over three hundred people after his resurrection, just as the Holy Bible records. You can write me off if you want, but if you want the only historically-accurate account of life after death, you have no choice that is better supported by factual evidence than to go to the Bible.

There is no shortcut around the fear of death. Either you're afraid to die, or you're not. And if you are, the only answer to this crippling fear that allows you to have peace and to function is faith. I say faith here and not education, because without first having faith in Christ, nothing you receive from educating yourself on what He has to say about death will matter. It'll be like the sound of rain over the ocean with no fishermen to hear. Empty.

FEAR OF THE UNCONTROLLABLE

As most people do, we eventually graduate out of our anxieties for Crap We Don't Understand because we go to school, or we're homeschooled, and we get educated about them. But while we are learning not to fear those things because we understand them, and in some capacity we can control them, we begin to learn about things that we can't control.

Microscopic organisms which want to wreck our insides and the only way to develop a resistance against them is to let the freaking menaces inside of us (how mental is that?!), and that the repercussion of not being resistant to these little crap heads is getting ill (the pain and suffering of which is often more scary than our previous prospect of dying. <Insert chicken pox memories here>). We learn that though we can control water to give us things to drink, to cook our food, or help us bathe or have fun, there are hurricanes and tsunamis. We learn about tornadoes and volcanoes and wildfires. Things that take those previous fears that we had overcome and make them extreme to the point that there is no control. The undertow of the ocean does not relent because you know how it works. Homes and forests don't reappear because we know that fire requires fuel and oxygen to burn. And water still scares the (insert favorite expletive here) out of me.

So how do we overcome our anxieties about these things? You're not going to like the answer any more than I do. But if I can overcome my fear of water enough to swim literally thousands of meters in a pool day after day, accept getting drowned over and over just to become comfortable with the idea of drowning, and take on so much water while sick that I got out of the pool, puked, and had the audacity to get back into that liquid evil, I'm sure you can handle this too. In a lot of ways, I'm sure you've already come to this conclusion; you may just not have realized it yet. The only way you overcome anxiety towards things you can't control is to accept them. That's it. You have to relinquish your desire for control and accept that there are things that God created that can and will absolutely wreck your face if you put yourself in a position to let them. Just like me and that stupid pool.

We're not done with this phase, though. There are two more categories that we still have to hit. The first is traumatic events. They're the ninja of life's anxieties because no one sees them coming, and sometimes we don't realize they happened until we're much older and dealing with the repercussions. I could write entire books on traumatic events in our lives. Better men and women already have. Most fiction of any genre is based on these things, and I'll say that fiction does a better job of revealing the hearts of people who experience trauma better than I ever could in this piece. Even if I tried, there are some things we experience that there simply are not words for. I've dealt with my fair share. I'm sure you have too. In some ways, I'm still dealing with mine.

So how do we keep these Goliaths from ruining our ability to function? I do it in three steps.

First, I always come back to community. Community will help with the other two steps and is necessary even before we realize we have the issue. If you don't have good people around you, your battle goes from being up hill to climbing Blood and Slaughter Mountain in a winter storm (I did it in the spring, and trust me, it was a feat even then). As a caveat to that, if you have toxic people in your life who are tearing you down as you try to recover, cut them out. I don't care who they are. Get rid of them. Having a toxic influence in your life while trying to heal from trauma takes your battle from climbing Blood and Slaughter Mountain in the winter and turns it into reaching the moon by using a pogo stick.

Second, you have to identify that the trauma exists. This might be obvious in some cases, but not so much in others.

That's where the community can help. Some people think they don't have a problem and don't actually need help. Some people think they need help with everything, when they really just need to pull themselves up by their bootstraps and move the hell on. Having a good community around you will help you find the happy medium.

Lastly, once you identify the problem, you have to accept it. This doesn't mean that it defines you, but it does become part of your identity. It does not mean "this trauma is who I am," but rather "this is part of what I have had to overcome." Some traumas will be harder to accept than others, and if it is severe, seek help. Whatever Christian started the whole movement of "you shouldn't see a therapist, you're just not believing or praying hard enough" needs to have the ever-loving crap slapped out of them. The ability to help someone heal mentally is a gift from God. To those who have this gift and choose to go into the field of therapy, I commend you, and as a community we should accept and use the tools God has provided us with to heal. Don't be a basket-case and go to your therapist every time you mess up your mom's chicken noodle soup recipe (as traumatizing as I know that is), but don't be ashamed to get help when you need it, either. Like I said before, there is a balance to this thing.

PERFORMANCE ANXIETY

Though we develop this anxiety at the same age as the things we can't control, I wanted to cover it separately, because unlike trauma and the natural things we discussed before, performance anxiety has a very different answer to it. The coward likes to use this anxiety to promote procrastination. It likes to manipulate our minds to psych us out and make us think that the expectations placed on us are unreasonably high. Worst of all the coward, will use it to shell-shock us for all eternity, convincing us that our gift isn't worth using because it's not worth failing if we try. Thus, we end up taking our gifts to the grave. No one remembers our name save for those who see our tombstone, and after a time, even that loses its meaning. Not because you weren't good enough for greatness, but because you simply didn't try.

The answer to performance anxiety? There are two.

Answer 1: knuckle down and do it. Do it over and over and over again. This seems like a "duh-huh" kind of solution, but it works. Most people have trouble with this due to a mental block. Answer two gets us past that block.

Answer 2: Change your reason for doing things. Most of the time I see people with performance anxiety, it's because they are scared of failure or scared they won't meet the expected performance quota. Screw the quota. You were given a gift. The only way you don't meet the quota on your gift is if you never use it. If that means using it because you're like me and you believe God mandated that you put that gift back into the world, use it. If you don't believe in God but you want to see what your gift becomes for you; use it. If it means setting a good example for your daughter so that she doesn't grow up with the same anxiety you have, use it. If it's for your ailing mother to whom you want to show your gift before she passes on, use it.

Whatever your gift is, it's worth finding so that you can kick the coward in the teeth and get back to what matters: using your gift.

ATTACKS ON OUR PRIDE

Piggy-backing off of performance anxiety, we often develop anxieties based on what others think of us. This leads to fears of negative evaluations and, the most common fear in high school-age kids, peer rejection.

I'll be frank with you when I say my empathy for the fear of a negative evaluation is extremely low. I just can't relate. What I can do, though, is share my mindset on why it doesn't bother me.

When was the last time you were able to grow by having someone tell you that you're perfect? If all you were ever told was "You're great! You're amazing!", do you think you would ever actually grow? Would you ever get better? Would you even want to continue doing whatever it is that you were trying at? There's an innate part of us as humans which desires a challenge. We love the feeling of overcoming a struggle and beating something that at one point had us stumped. I like to call this the Sherlock Holmes Effect. No matter how hard the problem, Holmes always strives for the answer, and it's not always out of a desire for justice, but also for the thrill of beating something difficult. We resonate with Holmes because there's a part of Holmes that is captured inside all of us. But when we remove negative evaluations from our lives, especially when they pertain to our gifts, we remove a struggle that we get to overcome. We remove part of the puzzle of life, the part that sits in the back of our minds and says, "How do I get better?" Negative evaluations, also known as critiques, are your road map to this answer. The coward would make you fear them so that you don't press forward and realize your potential. A champion overcomes this, lets the meaningless crap (because there will be some) roll off their back because it's not a bullet and it won't kill you, take what you can from each negative encounter to become better, and move on. Only when you linger in the negative does it become toxic. That's where the coward wants you, because that's where they win. Screw the coward. Move on.

Peer rejection is something quite different, though. Getting negative feedback or a negative evaluation from those whose opinions we value will hurt, but it'll make you better. Rejection from those people is something that hurts like hell, however. This one I feel you on, and I'm right there with you. I don't often put too much stock in what other people think. My experiences in grade school made me get over that. A story for a different day. But when I do put my stock in people, the magnitude of influence their opinions have on my life is massive. So, when I get rejected by such an individual, it can lead to some dark places.

One of the worst examples I can think of happened with an ex-girlfriend of mine. We had been together for about 3 years. My football life had slowed down a bit, it wasn't hunting season anymore, and I was looking to explore a new hobby. Actually, it was more like re-discovering a hobby; I was going to pick up dancing again. My girlfriend had never danced, but she was a musician of sorts, so I thought I would take a few lessons, see how I liked it, and then ask her to join me if it wasn't too bad. Considering my business history, you can assume how that went. After about three weeks of loving the lessons, I brought it up to my girlfriend, who responded, "That's so stupid. Why would you want to do that?"

I mark that as the beginning of the end for that romance, as well as a pivotal singularity in my life. Due to the lingering anxiety from that interaction, along with some opinions formed in maturity since then, I can count on one hand how many "Non-dancers" I have dated, all because I got rejected on the grounds of something I cared for deeply, by someone I cared for equally as much.

Much of my childhood was spent learning how to cope with

peer rejection. If there is any one anxiety I can speak to more than another, it's this one. It's also the hardest to cope with. Self-confidence helps, but it'll erode with time. Community helps, but you always run the risk of being rejected by those you build a community around. So, what gets us over this hill and allows us to keep trusting and loving and trying even when we've been hurt by rejection? Not to give you a wishy-washy answer here, but it's different for each person. I can only give you mine. If it makes sense, steal it. If not, search for your own. I support you either way. For me, though, I always come back to love. There is no greater act in this world than to share your heart with someone. This isn't just a romantic love (I envy the Greeks for having so many words for love, and the Chinese even more. They have like 50 or something) but it's a familial love, and as Professor Morrie Schwartz loved saying, "Love each other, or die."

DEPRESSION

I'm going to tell you something that I hope is comforting, but which goes against the culture. Just because you experience depression does not mean you are broken.

The common culture tells us that we're not allowed to be depressed. If we experience depression, we're not healthy, or we're broken. This is crap. Complete crap. As a matter of fact, telling people this makes them soft and weak and dependent. It's a reinforcement of what the coward wants you to believe. When the coward gets you in a place of depression, they want to keep you there. It's a place of control for the coward and the more you give into this idea that you're broken the longer the coward has to do irreparable damage.

Here's the secret sauce: experiencing depression, even near

suicidal depression, is a human experience. I have yet to meet a person who, when being completely honest with themselves, never went through a phase in their life where they didn't wonder, "Is it really worth it?" or "Am I really worth it?"

The answer is yes! Hell yes! You're worth it! You're worth all of it and more of it and then some. From a biblical perspective, you're so worth it that God sent a literal part of Himself to die for you because you're so worth it.

I know this stark truth may be hard to swallow, especially if you're in that place right now. But please understand this: you're not broken. You're human. This is part of being human, and I know it's not glamorous or fun, but it will make you strong. I know this because I've been there. I've been in that place where I've hurt so bad in my chest that I've wanted to die. I've been down that road where you wonder if life is worth living at all. It's a place where it's hard to get out of bed because there's nothing to look forward to in your life, a place where the things you love lose their value. For me it was my writing, and dancing, and reading. For you, it could be your art, or singing, a sport you play, or a group of people you like to spend time with. They lose their luster, and even chasing after God begins to look bleak, though you know He may be your only way out. It's a hopeless, barren wasteland packed to the brim with disappointment and fatigue.

One of the wonderful things about being human is that we get such a range of experiences through an extremely simple existence. At the end of the day, all we need to survive is food, water and a place to use as a toilet. Yet we have the capacity to find meaning, build relationships, and have experiences. Like I said before, depression isn't sexy, but it's real and it's a part of the human experience. We can make the choice to give into the despair and stay there forever, or we can view that despair as an opportunity to grow. It's up to us to make this choice. How we make it is different for everyone. I lean on God. You might use your family, or your friends, or your job. It might be your gift that pulls you through. Whatever it is, I beg you to find it, because this world needs you, and you're worth it. All the hurt, all the pain, all the disappointment. It's the fire that prepares you to be forged into a blade sharp enough to leave an indelible mark on this world. The forging happens in your mind. Make the choice. Strike the blade. Forge your psyche into who you want to become. Don't settle for who the world tries to tell you that you have to be.

And, as always, do everything you can to surround yourself with positive influences and optimistic people in your life. They're the ones who will remind you of your worth and value more often than this book ever could.

I kept this part short for a reason: mainly, that I'm not a psychologist. I genuinely believe that most people don't need one to face their depression, myself being one of those people, but I am also not naive enough to say that no one needs a doctor or professional help. There is a difference between minor thoughts of "Is life worth it?" and "I am going to kill myself, and here is how." The former line of thought can, if not plugged into a community or left unchecked, lead to the latter. I challenge you to find your strength internally and through your community first. However, should you find yourself on the latter path, please seek professional help sooner rather than later. God has gifted people with the ability to help you. Find one and do what needs to be done to stay with us so that you too can share your gift too.

FEAR

What are you afraid of?

If you're anything like me, you have a bevy of fears just boiling under your skin. They lead to anxiety, which leads to depression, so I put fear last because it is the catalyst. Anxiety and depression are just byproducts of fear. The coward inside of us feeds on fear so it can give rise to those other hellholes that we have to constantly dig ourselves out of. But what if we could keep from getting in those holes in the first place? What if there was a way to conquer fear?

Sorry to tease you, but the reality is that there isn't one. There is no magic formula, secret potion, energy rock or prayer that is going to completely remove fear.

That doesn't mean give up, though. That doesn't mean the coward gets to win. I used to hear this saying all the time about "fighting the good fight" and I never really knew what it meant. In all honesty, I still don't know exactly what it means, but if I had to guess, it would be this: fighting a fight that you know you cannot win but you cannot afford to lose. So, you keep fighting, even if it's only to keep the enemy at bay. If so, then I fight the good fight daily.

Now you might be thinking, "But Chad, you're so cool! You've founded a company, and served in the military, and have awesome nieces, and a cool brother, and awesome friends! What is there to be scared about?" Okay, you weren't thinking that, but a guy can dream.

The sad truth is that I'm more afraid now than I think I have ever been in my life. My fears range from professional to personal, and if you'll indulge me, I'll get personal and share them with you.

I'm scared of letting down those that I'm leading because their livelihoods depend on my leadership and direction. I'm scared that I've misread God's plan and path for my life. I'm scared I'll lose myself in my own ambition and lose the opportunity to experience great things in life, like love and a family. I'm scared of living a life that ends one day where I'm surrounded by the ghosts of opportunities I passed up because I was too afraid. I'm scared of seeing the faces of those who I could have helped but didn't because fear got the better of me. But the thing I fear the most? Disappointing God. I am scared of standing before my creator and hearing him say, "What happened? I gave you so many chances. I gave you so many opportunities. You completely missed the point."

So, I ask again. What are you afraid of?

You may have noticed that some of my greatest worries dealt with regret due to fear. I am scared of being hindered by my fear. It seems a tad oxymoronic, but when you make the choice to crush the coward, it's the only way to think.

When I read that President Kennedy said, "The only thing we have to fear is fear itself," I thought he was a lunatic pulling some snazzy political rhetoric to excite the crowd but which didn't have any real meaning. Then I thought about my own fears, how I'm afraid of fear in certain ways, and thought, "Maybe Kennedy was on to something."

Then I took it a step farther.

To beat the coward, I don't need to fear my fears. I need to embrace my fears. I need to acknowledge them. I need to live in them. I need to accept them as part of me and, rather than run from them, I need to harness my fear and use it as fuel. The coward isn't the only one that can be fueled by fear, but rather than the outcome be debilitating, I'll make sure the outcome makes me move forward. This change in my mindset showed me the truth behind the old saying, "there are few motivators quite like fear."

The more I turned my fear into fuel for action, the less afraid I felt. The more I acknowledged my fear and asked, "Okay, what can I do about this *today*," the less fear kept a hold on my life. I was also more productive and happier in general.

This led me to a new point that I want you to think about.

Don't be afraid of fear. Be afraid of a life without fear. The moment you stop experiencing fear is the moment you know you have nothing left to live for because you have nothing left to lose. So, fear the absence of fear, and fight daily to feed into the people and things you love so that you have something worth being afraid of losing.

I want you to learn to love the fear. I want you to learn to be deathly afraid of failure. I want you to be so scared of failure that failure is no longer an option.

There's a nuance with this as well, though. Failure doesn't mean what you think it means. I learned from my father that "failure isn't trying and not succeeding. Failure is having never tried at all." He's right, in a certain capacity. If not succeeding was failure, then I've failed at almost everything I've ever tried in my life. I flunked out of college my first time through, I dropped out of division one football, I failed at being a good employee and got fired, I failed at being a business owner on my first try, I failed the Tactical Air Control Party schoolhouse, I've failed more relationships than I care to count, and there are times where I feel like I've failed my family for not having my crap together sooner. I've failed as a leader. Worst of all, I fail God daily. Yet out of every failure, there was and is a lesson to be learned. I grew through trial and pain and hardship so I can sit here and type this with confidence. My dad's words have been the best combative to the fear of failure I have ever found, but I want to take it a step further. My dad's phrase focuses very much on the action. I want to take it to the thoughts that lead you to take action.

These thoughts that precede action, they typically come from a place of ambition and dreams. Especially if we're talking about using our gifts. You could be gifted with attention to detail and want to be a craftsman of some type. You could have a knack for rhythm and want to be a professional dancer or percussionist. You might be super acrobatic and have made it your dream to be part of Cirque du Soleil. Whatever it is, it starts with a dream. That dream compels you to act. You might fail, or fall, or have ten-to-many setbacks. That's okay. So long as you don't lose that ambition, you haven't lost the battle to the coward yet. You've still got him at bay, even if you haven't acted on those dreams yet. Why?

Dad said, "Failure isn't trying and not succeeding. Failure is never trying at all."

I say, "True failure is the hopelessness that comes when you give up your capacity to dream." In other words, you fail when you abandon your gift.

The fastest way the enemy can convince you to walk away from that gift is through fear.

Though I believe this is the first step crushing the coward, I put it last because I want it to sink in for you. Please, if you got nothing else out of this chapter, hear me when I say this: the acknowledgment of fear is not weakness or submission. It is the first step to crushing the coward.

"I learned that courage was not the absence of fear, but the triumph over it. The brave man is not he who does not feel afraid, but he who conquers that fear."

- Nelson Mandela

JUMP THE GUN

ear, anxiety, and depression are part of being human. Without them, we can't honestly experience what it means to be
alive.

But they should never rule over us. They should never
keep you from stepping out and using your gifts. Yet, as we've
covered, the coward will attempt to marshal these experiences
against you and forge them into a cage, or worse a noose.

Though we've covered a lot with these topics, there is one
method that I find more useful than any other in crushing the
coward, and that is crushing it before it can ever take root in
yourself. I liken this tactic to racing. Whether it be at a swim
meet for the 100 meter, a track meet for the 400 relay, or the
drag strip for the next quarter mile, there is a phrase used when
people start early: jumping the gun. In the instance of a race,
it's considered cheating to jump the gun because you started
the race with an unfair advantage over your opponent. In life,
there is no such thing as an unfair advantage. Some people
will tell you that any advantage is unfair and that you should
pay for any advantage you were given because other people
might not have had that advantage. I say screw that. Life is
hard, and as long as you are acting with integrity and morality,
you should take every advantage you can get and then use your
success to provide advantages and opportunities to other people. But when it comes to your personal mental health, when

it's just you and the coward fighting over who wins the war for your mind, all bets are off. Fight dirty against the coward. Take every advantage, however you can, and do not relent when the coward attempts to get hold. Claw, kick, scream, and gouge out the eyes of the coward and let your courage be seen. Do it before the coward can ever see it coming. Train yourself to get ahead of the coward, to beat it before it knows what hit them.

In other words, jump the gun.

How? I've found one sure fire way in my own life. Do one thing every day that makes you uncomfortable. It doesn't have to be big. It could be as simple as going for a run, or killing a bug. It could be as extreme as spending days on a camping trip alone to see how you handle it, or going skydiving if you're afraid of heights. By proving you can do something external that makes you uncomfortable you become better equipped to handle what happens to us internally. C.S. Lewis says it best in the *Screwtape Letters* when he reminds us that we're animals, and what we do physically affects the state of our souls. Strengthen your mind toward the outside world and you'll naturally become stronger when facing the internal struggles life presents. You have to do it now, though, before the coward gets its grimy claws in you. It's much harder to get ahead if you're starting from behind.

GREATNESS IS EASY

Though a short book, there is a lot here to unpack. Please, as you need to throughout your life, go back and re-read it. I wrote this as a highlight of the things I love to talk about in my professional life, but also as a guide for anyone who feels a bit lost in the swamp of our current society. The guide, though densely packed, is pretty easy to follow. As you follow it, I'm sure you'll find ways to make it your own.

But remember this: even when life gets hard, greatness is easy. Greatness is easy because so many people in this world are satisfied with being mediocre and the world is more than willing to reward that mediocrity. You don't have to be gifted in such a way that it allows you to do something no one else has ever done. Rather, be willing to work harder and give more effort than anyone else is willing to give.

THE MESSAGE

"You were not sent here merely to receive! You were sent here to give."
-Dr. Miles Monroe

I'm going to take this opportunity to be beat a dead horse one last time.

The gifts you're carrying? They're not for you. That passion in your belly? It's not for you. That desire for success? *It is not for you.*

God did not give us our gifts to be coveted. They were not given to us so that we could carry them and dream about them and then let them die with us. The treasures residing in your mind, born of the passion placed on your heart, that could one day be the product of the work of your hands, were not meant for you.

They were meant for the world. Give it back. Dream, think, build, create! But create for the world. Give unto others that gift that you have. Inspire people with your generosity, your hard work, your dedication, and let someone else reap the benefit of your labor. Let them hear your music. Let them see your art. Let them read your book. Let hear your story, be touched by your leadership, or be saved by your courage.

Regardless of what your gift might be, who it might touch, or what it might create, I pray with all my heart that you do not take it to the grave. Live such a life that you don't need a tombstone.

Give unto others, that others may give.

ACKNOWLEDGEMENTS

When I set out to become an author at the age of eight, never did I imagine that this would be my first book. I dreamed it would be a fantasy novel, something cliché that mirrored the great epics I grew up reading while also managing to be just original enough for a company to pick it up. Never did I imagine that it would be my own company that published this book. Never would it have been possible without the following people:

To my Mother: Thank you teaching me countless lessons on perseverance, business, compassion, and reality.

To my Father: Thank you for showing me what it means to be a man, for teaching me that if you're going to do something to do it right, but never get so wrapped up in perfection that you fail to do anything at all. Hustle, play hard, play fast.

To Dr. Monroe: Though I will not meet you till I arrive at the pearly gates know your work, your words, and your mission live on in me.

To Brianna: I thank God daily that you entered my life. Forerunner Publications would not be possible without you.

To Andre: For helping convince me to take a leap of faith that led down this path. Love you brother.

To Chase: Though audio has nothing to do with this, thank you for being my secret weapon and an incredible friend. Your role is too much for words.

To Sabrina and Zach: To write is human. To edit is divine. You made this book better and more accessible to our audience. Thank you.

To my Beta-readers: Christian, Jason, Brianna, Chase, Andre, and Cheryl, thank you for dealing with early draft of this book and helping to become what it has. You gave me confidence to take this to the next step.

To Kyle: Your memory lives on.

SUGGESTED READING

I wanted to include a list of books that have made a dramatic impact on my life and lead to many of the thoughts compiled in this short book. While some are cited in this book, others will appear to have zero relevance. This list encompasses the thoughts and ideas of others which have shaped me to who I am. Therefore, each one is important to the writing of this book as those directly cited. I hope you find each of them as enlightening as I do.

21 Indispensable Qualities of a Leader by John C. Maxwell
The Alchemist by Paulo Coelho
The Abolition of Man by C.S. Lewis
The Anatomy of Story by John Truby
Genesis by Moses/God (King James Version)
The Count of Monte Cristo by Alexander Dumas
Ender's Game by Orson Scott Card
Fallen Angels by Walter Dean Myers
The Giver by Lois Lowry
The Iliad by Homer (Alexander Pope or Robert Fagles Translation)
Leaders Eat Last by Simon Sinek
The Lord of the Rings by J.R.R. Tolkien
Man's Search for Meaning by Victor E. Frankl
On Writing by Steven King

Pride and Prejudice by Jane Austin
The Screwtape Letters by C.S. Lewis
Story by Robert McKee
Sun Stand Still by Steven Furtick
Tuesdays with Morrie by Mitch Albom
Under a War-Torn Sky by L.M. Elliot
The Wise Man's Fear by Patrick Rothfuss

ABOUT THE AUTHOR

Chad W. Garrett is the Executive Producer of Forerunner Productions and its subsidiary Forerunner Publications. When not writing or running his company he can be found serving the United States Air Force, rock climbing, hiking, or dancing. His greatest passion is analyzing the narratives that have shaped our world, understanding them and their implications toward our future, and educating others not only on what he finds but on how to find these lessons for themselves.